Think Math!

Interactive Loops for Groups

Dale Bulla

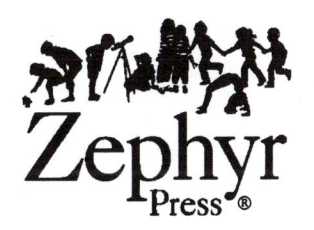

Zephyr Press®

Reaching Their Highest Potential
Tucson, Arizona

Think Math!
Interactive Loops for Groups
Grades 4–8

© 1996 by Zephyr Press
Printed in the United States of America

ISBN 1-56976-027-6

Editors: Stacey Lynn and Stacey Shropshire
Cover design: Nancy Taylor
Design and production: Daniel Miedaner

Zephyr Press
P.O. Box 66006
Tucson, Arizona 85728-6006

All rights reserved. The purchase of this book entitles the individual teacher to reproduce the forms for use in the classroom. The reproduction of any part for an entire school or school system or for commercial use is strictly prohibited. No form of this work may be reproduced, transmitted, or recorded without written permission from the publisher.

Library of Congress Cataloging-in-Publication Data
  Bulla, Dale.
    Think math! : interactive loops for groups / Dale Bulla.
      p. cm.
    ISBN 1-56976-027-6
    1. Mathematics—Study and teaching (Elementary) I. Title.
  QA135.5.B82 1996   95-13799
  372.7'044—dc20

---

*Thanks to my wife, Pat,
without whose patience and editing
this book would have never been finished.
And special thanks to Brad Newton
and the following students:*

Misty Greene
Charlotte Whitfield
Jordan Jackson

Contents

Introduction	1
1. What Is a Loop?	3
The Loop Process	4
How Does It Work?	6
2. Making Math Loops	13
Variations of the Math Loop	13
What Essential Elements Does the Math Loop Contain?	14
Math vs Arithmetic	20
What If the Loop Doesn't Work?	21
3. Related Issues	23
Risk Taking	23
Creative Mathematics	26
4. Mental Gymnastics	28
5. Sample Math Loops	30
Loop A: Addition and Subtraction	31
Loop B: Addition, Subtraction, and Multiplication	34
Loop C: Addition, Subtraction, Multiplication, and Division	37
Loop D: Includes Fractions	40
Loop E: Includes Squares, Square Roots, Cubes, and Cube Roots	43
Loop F: Includes Algebra, Geometry, and Math Terms	46
6. Sample Loops for Language Arts	50
Loop A: Parts of Speech, Grammar, and Punctuation	51
Loop B: Synonyms and Antonyms	54
7. Sample Social Studies Loop	57
8. Sample Science Loop	60
9. Sample Loop for Multiple Content Areas	63

Contents

10.	**Sample Problem Solving Activities**	66
	How Tall Is the School?	66
	Building a Scale Model of the Solar System	68
	Horses and Zebras	70
	How Did It Do That?	72
	The Magic of Nine	75
	Magic Number Squares	76
11.	**Math Loops for Grade Four**	78
12.	**Math Loops for Grade Five**	91
13.	**Math Loops for Grade Six**	104
14.	**Math Loops for Grades Seven and Eight**	117
15.	**Geometry Loops**	139
16.	**Algebra Loops**	146

Introduction

This book contains ideas, activities, and a personal philosophy that worked well for me during my twenty years of teaching. Many of the concepts provided here have been adapted from ideas that resulted from interactions with students, teachers, and others. Now I am a private consultant, and my workshop participants tell me of their success using these techniques with students year after year. However, I do not consider myself to be an expert.

Those of us who have been teaching for ten years or longer know that there is really no such thing as an expert in education. If we really had experts, we would have figured out the best ways of dealing with children long ago. The reason that has not happened is that kids are constantly changing. As soon as we think we have them figured out, one will come along and blow away all our theories.

In addition, the curriculum is always changing. As soon as teachers work the bugs out of a curriculum, it changes. So teachers never feel they get enough practice with a curriculum to be proficient with the objectives.

And finally, we as teachers are changing. We are always refining our skills and increasing our knowledge. Change is constant and inevitable. I believe that when we recognize this fact, we can let go and create what is best for our students at this time and in this place. We also have to believe in ourselves. We must believe that we know best how to challenge our students. And with the help of supportive supervisors and administrators, we can continue to do what we do best—teach.

I hope the information presented here will provide you with new ideas and at the same time encourage you to create and adapt. My goal is to stimulate your creativity to discover new ways of problem solving while validating the concept that teaching, as well as learning, can still be fun!

1
What Is a Loop?

A loop is something that goes around and comes back to where it began. Loops are often associated with computer programs. By linking commands that depend on the previous commands, we can establish a loop. The program then runs in sequence and continues to run because the last command refers back to the first command. Once started, the program will run continuously until the plug is pulled, it reaches an end to the conditions set in the loop, or the operator hits the escape button.

The math loop, which is made up of arithmetic operations, works in a similar way. I have designed the loop as a practice tool that uses operations with which the student is already familiar. You should seldom use loops to teach new concepts.

One of the great benefits of the math loop is that it allows students to practice routine operations without getting bored. Students may dislike math or arithmetic drill because of the laborious repetition. Elementary classrooms often begin the year with page after page of addition, subtraction, multiplication, or division problems. The pretest in a text may use work sheets or workbook pages to find out if students remember their "math facts." Frequently students have an aversion to these pages, and they make comments such as, "We did these last year." "Do we have to do these again?"

Instead of starting off the year with a classroom full of students who are resistant to repetitive tasks or who write down any answers to be finished quickly with a rote activity, why not start the year differently? Why not try math loops? Suppose as the teacher of a third-grade math class, you want to discover what your students remember about math operations. Give them the math loop on page 5.

> **You may have to ask those who want to yell out the answer to be patient while enjoying the excitement that this activity generates.**

Copy page 5. Cut the answers and questions into ten strips and mount them on note cards or just give them to any ten students. Pass them out in any order. Explain to students that if they don't have a strip, they will get one next time. To get more students involved, have students look on with neighbors or work with partners. Of course some students will be listening and discovering the answers in their heads. You may have to ask those who want to yell out the answer to be patient and enjoy the excitement that this activity generates.

The Loop Process

You might want to say something like, "The object is to listen to what is being read and look at your sentence to see if you have the correct answer. If your sentence has the correct answer to the question read, then raise your hand and I will call on you." Or you may just let the one who thinks she or he has the right answer read it aloud. To begin the loop, you could ask, "Who would like to read your sentence first?"

When you choose a student, the loop begins. For example, the first student might read, "I have 0. Who has 3 more than I have?" The student with the strip that says "I have 3. Who has this and 7 more?" responds next. Of course the answer is, "I have 10 . . . " and so on. The loop continues until each person with a strip has participated. The loop comes back to the one who began it after someone reads the strip that says "I have 7. Who has this take away 7?" The student with zero is the one who read first. The loop has now been completed and the students will readily recognize the end.

Some student might ask, "How did it do that?" Your response could be, "Magic!" or, "Would you like to learn how to make one?" Or you might say, "I don't know. Let's give the sentences to other people and try it again to see what happens."

I have 10. *Who has 2 more than I do?*	**I have 9.** *Who has two less than this, minus two more?*
I have 12. *Who has 6 less than I have?*	**I have 5.** *Who has three less than I do, plus 5?*
I have 6. *Who has this plus 2?*	**I have 7.** *Who has this take away 7?*
I have 8. *Who has this minus 4?*	**I have 0.** *Who has 3 more than I have?*
I have 4. *Who has this and 5 more?*	**I have 3.** *Who has this and 7 more?*

Think Math! © 1995 Zephyr Press, Tucson, AZ

This time give the cards or strips to students who didn't participate the first time. Ask for a volunteer again and let the loop run. The results are the same in the sense that the loop will come back to the one who started it. Encourage students to talk about what they observe. Let them hypothesize. Let them problem solve.

How Does It Work?

After you have given students the opportunity to try a loop or two, someone may ask, "Can we make one?" The answer is, "Of course you can." You might say, "Who would like to make a loop?" Usually hands go up around the room when I ask this question. It is always enjoyable for students to be involved in the process of creating loops.

It is easy to demonstrate how the loop is made. Use the chalkboard or an overhead projector with transparencies to do the following.

Draw a vertical line down the middle of the chalkboard or the transparency and put a horizontal line near the top (see figure 2-1). The space to the left of the vertical line is called the "I have . . ." side, and the space to the right is the "Who has . . . ?" side.

Next ask if someone would like to pick a number—any number. Suppose a student chooses the number 20. Write this on the left, or the "I have," side. Then ask for another number, a different number. Perhaps someone calls out the number 6. Write 6 under the number 20 on the left side. Now the diagram looks something like that shown in figure 2-2.

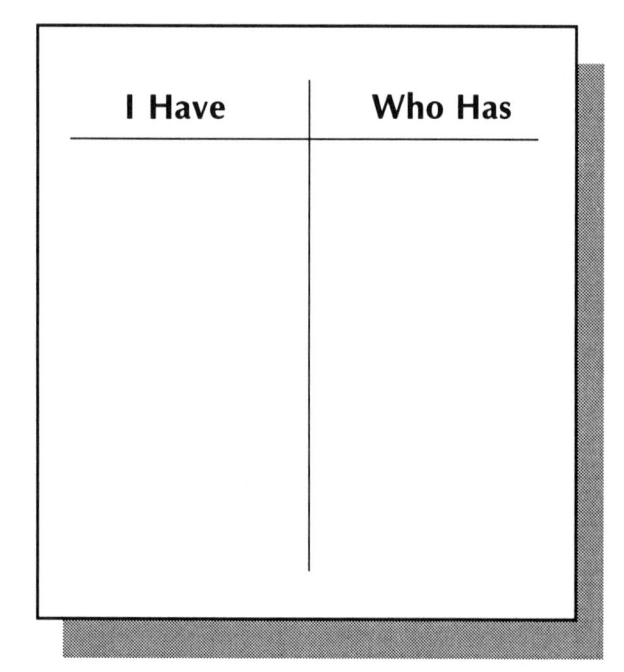

Figure 2-1. *The diagram for beginning a math loop*

Now ask if anyone has an idea about how to get from 20 to 6 using a math/arithmetic operation. A student might say, "Minus 14." If so, you could ask, "Is that the only way?" Someone might say, "Minus 10 and minus 4 more" or, "Take away 20 and add 6." Let the class brainstorm other ways to get from 20 to 6 using math operations. All the answers may be correct and yet the operations to arrive at the correct answer may be quite varied.

Some students may not be accustomed to having multiple solutions to a math problem, so this is a great time to talk about *risk taking* and *creative mathematics*. (See chapters 7 and 8 for a discussion of these ideas.)

I Have	Who Has
20	
6	

▲ *Figure 2-2.* The "I Have . . ." side partially filled in

I Have	Who Has
20	this minus 14?
6	

▲ *Figure 2-3.* Beginning to fill in the "Who Has . . . ?" side

Now select one of the operations given by a student and place that solution on the right side of the diagram directly across from the number 20. Now the diagram looks similar to that shown in figure 2-3.

Now ask for another number, a different number. It is important that none of the numbers on the left side be duplicated, because duplication will break the loop; two card holders will have the correct answer to one of the questions.

What Is a Loop?

Perhaps someone now calls out 8. Write the number 8 on the left side under the number 6, and then ask how to get from 6 to 8 using math/arithmetic operations. Someone may say, "Add 2" or, "Plus 2" or, "2 more." Someone may even say, "Add 4, minus 2." Each operation gives the correct final answer and yet the methods are different. Reward the diverse responses. It is important to create an environment early in the year that encourages and rewards risk taking. Try some of these responses to students who take risks:

Oh, I love that answer.
Wow! I never have heard that before.
I'm glad you're in my class.
I love to have students like you.
It's great when people take a chance.
I think risk takers are special.

I Have	Who Has
20	this minus 14?
6	this and 2 more?
8	

▲ **Figure 2-4.** *The math loop continues*

Even if the answers are wrong, thank students for trying and help them discover their "thinking errors." Thinking errors are okay. Adults know that mistakes are part of everyday life. A student, however, may be humiliated by a public *faux pas*. In fact, some students would rather be silent than make a mistake, especially in public. These students are prime candidates for "tuning out." As teachers, we must constantly reinforce the idea that people learn from mistakes. Without errors, no one makes progress. Youngsters must be like turtles, who make progress only by sticking their necks out.

The diagram now looks similar to that shown in figure 2-4.

I Have	Who Has
20	this minus 14?
6	this and 2 more?
8	this take away 3?
5	

▲ *Figure 2-5.* The next answer is added to the loop

Get another number, for example, 5. Put 5 under the 8 and ask students to tell how to get from 8 to 5. Maybe "Take away 3" is the answer you select. Write "Take away 3" on the right side directly across from the 8 so that your chart looks something like that shown in figure 2-5.

Again ask for another number. Let's say the next number is 2. Place the 2 under the 5 and ask how to get from 5 to 2. Someone may suggest that 2 is 3 less than 5, so write "3 less than this" to the right of the 5 and call for another number.

The diagram now looks something like that shown in figure 2-6.

I Have	Who Has
20	this minus 14?
6	this and 2 more?
8	this take away 3?
5	3 less than this?
2	

▲ *Figure 2-6.* Add another answer and question

What Is a Loop?

I Have	Who Has
20	this minus 14?
6	this and 2 more?
8	this take away 3?
5	3 less than this?
2	this plus 10 and 8 more?

▲ *Figure 2-7.* The loop ends

At this point, tell students that they are making a small loop just for practice and that it is time to end this loop. For the loop to work correctly, the last operation must give an answer that is equal to the number with which the loop began. Ask students for ideas about how to get from 2 back to 20, since 20 is the beginning number. After brainstorming ways to get to 20, select one operation and place it on the right side across from the number 2.

The diagram will now look something like that shown in figure 2-7.

This completes the process for making a five-card loop. You can easily see what to write on each of the five cards or strips if you now draw horizontal lines across the diagram. Number each line on the diagram for the demonstration, but tell students you will *not* number the final cards and they will not number the cards or strips they create. Doing so would give too much of a hint about the sequence of the cards.

The final diagram now looks something like that shown in figure 2-8.

I Have		Who Has
card 1	20	this minus 14?
card 2	6	this and 2 more?
card 3	8	this take away 3?
card 4	5	3 less than this?
card 5	2	this plus 10 and 8 more?

▲ *Figure 2-8.* The diagram with the cards numbered

How Does It Work?

The next step is to transfer the information from the working diagram to individual cards. Give each student five blank cards or have them cut out five strips of paper. Demonstrate what should be written on card number one.

It should say: ▶

> **I have 20.**
>
> *Who has this minus 14?*

Card number two should say: ▶

> **I have 6.**
>
> *Who has this and 2 more?*

Card number three should say: ▶

> **I have 8.**
>
> *Who has this take away 3?*

Card number four should say: ▶

> **I have 5.**
>
> *Who has 3 less than this?*

And card number five should say: ▶

> **I have 2.**
>
> *Who has this plus 10 and 8 more?*

What Is a Loop?

> **Emphasize to them, "Put your name on the back of each of your cards."**

When students have made their own five-card sets, ask them again not to number the cards but to put their names on the backs of their cards. Emphasize to them, "Put your name on the back of each of your cards." This way, if a couple of students drop their cards on the floor, it will not take forever to determine which cards go with which loop set. Also, insist that students save their practice diagrams for later—just in case someone's loop doesn't work. If this happens, the student can refer back to the diagram. Comparing the diagram to the cards is a good process for discovering the error.

Once the cards are ready, have students form groups of five. Let each group begin with one student's set of loop cards; that student should give each member of the group a card from his or her set. The practice round will let the student know if the loop works. Have students take turns until everyone in the group has practiced with each set of loops made by the members.

The goal is for your students to have learned the process of how loops work and how to construct them. At this point some students may be ready to branch out and create their own unique loops.

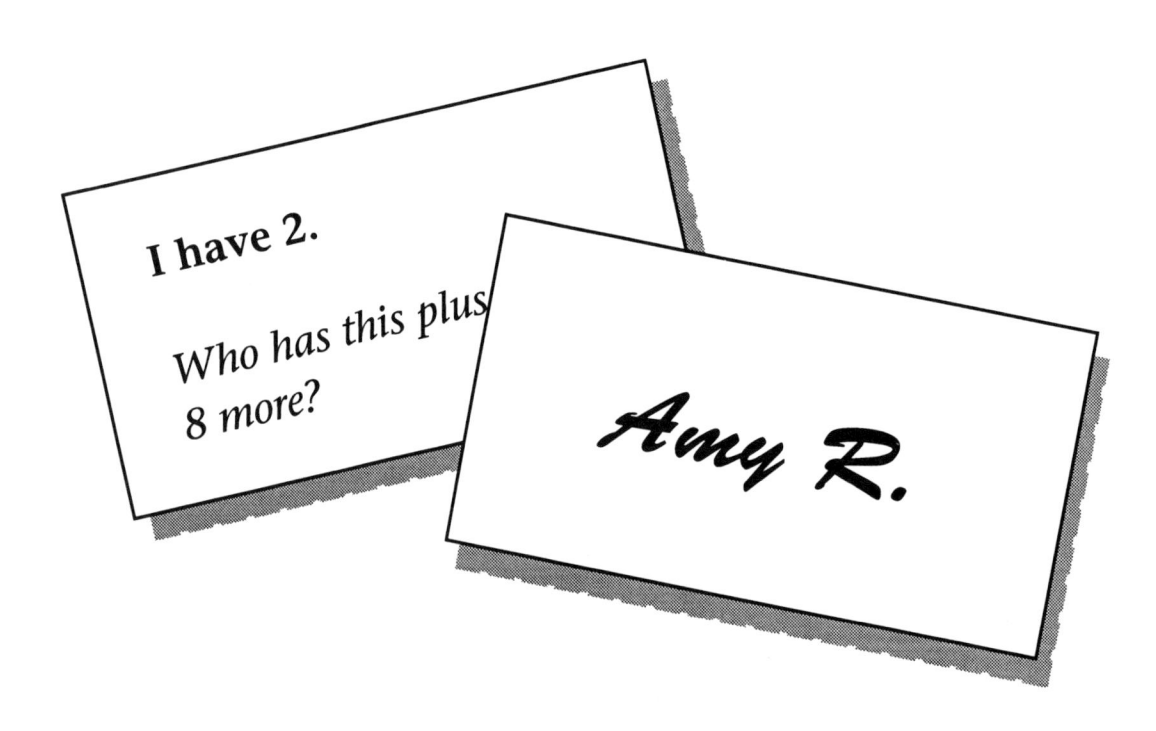

2
Making Math Loops

Variations of the Math Loop

Once students have mastered the basic loop-making technique, you can encourage them to create an incredible variety of loops using all types of mathematical operations. They can use addition and subtraction as well as multiplication and division, depending on the level of their knowledge and experience. Remember that loops work best when students use them to practice what they already know rather than to learn new material. Using what they know allows for individual differences while it stimulates the creative process.

Let students brainstorm the different ways in which they can use math loops and the variations of the different formats. Many students will come up with ideas that are more interesting and creative than the ones described here.

When a loop is running, the entire class should be involved in the activity. Therefore, it is best for each student in the room to have a card. In other words, if you have twenty-four students, the ideal loop will have twenty-four cards. Remind students that each number on the left side of the practice diagram must appear only once. If two cards have the same "I have" number, the loop will break. There will be two correct

> **Loops are a great "whole brain" activity because they allow for creating new thoughts in a light-hearted environment while using facts and logical operations.**

answers and no one will know which card to read.

On pages 15–17 is an example of a 24-card loop for fourth or fifth grade. You might want to start with this one for the initial class experience. If you have fewer than twenty-four students, let some have two cards. If you have more than twenty-four, let some share a card.

There will be students who enjoy the playfulness of this activity and who will make and bring to class loops that will surprise everyone. Enjoy this when it happens. For many students, math is not something that has ever been fun, so let them see that it can tickle their creativity bone.

I had a student one year who made enough cards so that everyone in the class had two cards and therefore two sets of answers and questions to look at. It was great to watch the kids looking back and forth at their cards, often asking for a repeat while they scanned both strips at once. Some students asked others to be quiet so they could concentrate. Of course some students were counting on their fingers or using a scrap of paper as a help, while others could handle the mental gymnastics easily.

Amusing and playful behavior helps the creative process to grow and thrive. Loops are a great "whole brain" activity because they allow for creating new thoughts in a light-hearted environment while using facts and logical operations. Loops not only let kids enjoy routine but make it more enjoyable for you as well.

What Essential Elements Does the Math Loop Contain?

It is often necessary for teachers to make notes in their lesson plans about the objectives or learning elements that an activity is either teaching or reinforcing. The additional strengths of the math loop are evident in this planning activity.

Remember, the purpose of loops is to allow your students to practice rote learning in a playful way while giving plenty of opportunity for students to internalize basic math operations. For this internalization to be accomplished, students need to understand loops well enough to be able to make their own. Look at the number of skills they must practice just to make a math loop.

Math Loop Variations

I have 40.	**I have 30.**
Who has half of this?	*Who has this and 6 more?*

I have 20.	**I have 36.**
Who has this and 1 more?	*Who has 1/6 of my number?*

I have 21.	**I have 6.**
Who has this divided by 7?	*Who has 1 less than I have?*

I have 3.	**I have 5.**
Who has this times 10?	*Who has this squared?*

Think Math! © 1995 Zephyr Press, Tucson, AZ

Math Loop Variations

I have 25.

Who has 4 times as much as I do?

I have 16.

Who has 1/8 of this?

I have 100.

Who has the square root of this?

I have 2.

Who has this to the fifth power?

I have 10.

Who has this plus 2, divided by 3?

I have 32.

Who has this plus 10?

I have 4.

Who has this times itself?

I have 42.

Who has double this?

Math Loop Variations

I have 84. *Who has this minus 10, plus 1?*	**I have 0.** *Who has this minus 12?*
I have 75. *Who has 1/3 of this, minus 4, divided by 3?*	**I have negative 12.** *Who has this plus 10?*
I have 7. *Who has 10 more than this?*	**I have negative 2.** *Who has this times 2?*
I have 17. *Who has this plus 3, divided by 5, minus 4?*	**I have negative 4.** *Who has this times negative 10?*

Handwriting Skills

For example, students write the cards after completing their practice diagrams, so they are getting plenty of opportunities to develop their handwriting skills. You can decide whether students should write the cards in cursive or manuscript depending on what you want to reinforce or have students practice.

Grammar and More

Students need to start each sentence with a capital and end it with a period or question mark. Students need to use appropriate sentence structure and grammar, as well as correct spelling, to create sentences that others can easily understand. Some students may even complain, "This is math. We shouldn't have to spell or punctuate in here." What a great opportunity to discuss compartmentalized learning. I like to point out to students that school is the only place in the world where the following happens: The bell rings at the end of language arts class and the students yell, "We don't have to do language the rest of the day."

> **In the everyday world, math, science, reading, and writing are used all day long.**

In the everyday world, math, science, reading, and writing are used all day long. When you go to the grocery store to buy a box of cereal, you not only need to be able to read the name of the cereal and the ingredients, but also to know how much is in the box. You probably also want to know the price and whether this box is a better buy than another one. You may also want to analyze the fat and sugar content to be sure you are taking good care of your body.

Integrate Subjects

Acquaint your students early with the multidisciplinary nature of learning. You can accomplish this feat more easily in the lower elementary grades where children stay with the same teacher most of the day. Units of instruction that integrate a variety of subjects can make learning more relevant and fun. In upper elementary and middle school when students start changing classes, they pick up the idea that math is used only between 10:00 and 10:50. Math loops help students see that successful students use all their skills whenever they need them regardless of the class in which they find themselves.

Depending on your teaching objective, you might incorporate many other goals into the math loop. Suppose a class is learning the difference between cardinal and ordinal numbers. Cardinal numbers may be written as numerals, such as 4, 5, 6, 7. They may also be written as number words, such as four, five, six, seven. Often students have plenty of practice with numerals but little practice with number words and ordinal numbers that show position in a series, such as fourth, fifth, sixth, seventh.

Math loops give students a perfect chance to use these words in context and with meaning rather than memorizing them for a test. In addition, note the other math words that can appear in math loops: more than, less than, greater than, half of, plus, subtracted, minus, times, divided, added to, take away, and so on.

> **Math loops give students a perfect chance to use these words in context and with meaning rather than memorizing them for a test.**

Whatever words or concepts the students are practicing or using can be put into a loop. For example, one week you might tell your students, "This week we are not going to write any numerals in our math loops. Instead we will practice all the number words we have been using in our spelling list."

Students often catch on quickly to math symbols (+, -, x, and so on). The loop is the place to see if students can also correctly use the words that these symbols represent. To use these words in sentences, students also need to spell them correctly, because other students will be reading the words.

As teachers, we often try to prevent failure in children by not allowing students to experience the consequences of their actions. Most students are accustomed to turning in papers that no person on earth but their teacher could decipher. Thus, many students deduce, "If my teacher can read it, it must be okay." Math loops give children a chance to be told by their peers, "I can't read this" or, "What is this word?" What better reason to improve handwriting than the fact that when it cannot be read, the loop won't work? All of a sudden there is a good reason to spell correctly and write legibly.

Additional Loop Benefits

These are a few of the essential elements that the loop provides for the maker. Now look at the benefits to the students who run the loop. In order to make the loop work, everyone has to listen. Listening skills are important for everyone. Obviously loops require students to read. They also require students to speak clearly so that others can understand.

Students practice listening for meaning each time a loop runs.

> Group dynamics, sharing, group interactions, and cooperative learning are important concepts in any classroom, and loops can help teachers meet their goals in these areas.

Group dynamics, sharing, group interactions, and cooperative learning are important concepts in any classroom, and loops can help teachers meet their goals in these areas. Loops get every student involved from the very beginning. If you start with the sample ten-card loop, then probably some students have no card. Even so, they may call out the answer when someone does not respond quickly. There may be a student who has the correct answer but is afraid to read his or her card. Perhaps that student is fearful it is wrong, until someone pokes him or her and says, "You've got it. Read it." Even if the student does not have the appropriate card, that student's mind is involved in the activity. Pairing or teaming students can often build a sense of cooperative learning that can also help develop students' self-esteem. Loops can also create a nurturing and caring environment that spills over into other content areas.

Loop races can also be great fun. After a loop has run successfully, have students get into teams and let them challenge each other. Let them take turns running a loop. Appoint a timekeeper to record how many minutes or seconds the loop takes. While one team is working, others can be monitoring the stopwatch. Have students use the notations for minutes and seconds. For example, team A = 2' 23" ("two minutes and twenty-three seconds"), and team B = 3' 10" ("three minutes and ten seconds"). The teams will be learning and practicing what you want them to know, and they will have fun while they learn and create.

Math vs Arithmetic

A math loop requires not only accurate calculations but, what is more important, knowledge of math operations. Without both types of skills, students cannot create successful loops. Some "math" classrooms are just arithmetic classrooms in disguise, especially in the lower grades. Students are taught to calculate and manipulate numbers, but they often don't understand number relationships or why specific operations succeed. The hows and whys of arithmetic are found in mathematics. Number lines and number charts show the *relationships* among numbers. Such insight goes beyond mere computation. The more young children are permitted and encouraged to problem solve and hypothesize, the better prepared they are to use mathematics in the future. If their sole motivation is to get the right answer, then they are being cheated out of the fun and creativity that mathematics can offer.

When a student sits down to tackle a group of word problems, how often is there a look of puzzlement on the student's face? Perhaps he or she asks, "Do I add or subtract, multiply or divide?" or sighs, "Just tell me what to do with the numbers and I can get the answer." Such comments come from arithmetic students, not math students. Math is a way of thinking. To approach a problem and be able to estimate the answer or predict the approximate outcome shows that good problem solving abilities are being developed. If students can enjoy this facet of math, they have a future in the real world of mathematics. Arithmetic is limited mainly to workbooks and textbooks and the chalkboards of American classrooms.

Some teachers don't feel that math is one of their strengths. Feelings of inadequacy or dislike may be transferred nonverbally to students. It is therefore essential that we as teachers demonstrate our willingness to take risks and make mistakes to model how difficulties can be overcome. If we always rely on the answer book, students will get a certain message from that behavior. When students see us try, fail, and try again, we send a stronger and more positive message than lecturing could ever give.

Problem solving and the use of logic can stimulate excitement about mathematics in students. Math games, puzzles, tangrams, and other playful ways of exposing kids to logical and mathematical thinking will help build the resilience and interest that are necessary to develop the mathematicians of the future.

> **When students see us try, fail, and try again, we send a stronger and more positive message than lecturing could ever give.**

What If the Loop Doesn't Work?

When you or your students have completed a loop and placed it on cards, the next logical step is to bring it to class and let it run. To validate the creative process, students should experience the success of their finished products. However, you should be prepared for many of the loops not to work. The reason quickly becomes evident as the specific problems are discovered. The most common mistake that students make is to copy the loop information incorrectly from the diagram format to the cards. Simple errors in transferring the information from one place to the other quickly become obvious when the loops run. You can expect this type of error to occur and use these mistakes as a chance to practice the risk taking that we need to encourage in students.

"Boss of the Loop" Technique

Try this technique before a loop breaks. When a student brings a loop to class to test, make that student the "boss of the loop." The boss will pass out the loop cards and select a student to begin reading. Suppose a child reads a card and no one seems to have the answer. You might ask the class what the answer is. Most students will know the answer because they will have been calculating in their heads. Some will look at their neighbors' cards to see if they can find the correct answer.

At this point it is not necessary to dwell on the fact that the loop isn't working; it is very evident that it is not. You can simply say to the boss, "Well your loop doesn't seem to be working today. Why don't you fix it, and we will try it again tomorrow? If you need some help troubleshooting, I will be glad to assist you, or you may ask someone else to help."

Always encourage students to find their own errors and learn from their mistakes.

The student will then collect the cards and compare them with the diagram of his or her loop. As I said, the most common mistake is a copying error. Perhaps the "I have" part of one card has been confused with the "Who has" part of another card. If the student discovers the error, meaningful learning takes place. Always encourage students to find their own errors and learn from their mistakes. After the corrections are made, always provide an opportunity for the student to try again to validate the loop's effectiveness.

Expect Delays

Too often as teachers, we dwell on failure and do not get around to the business of correcting the error. Often *who* makes the mistake is emphasized more than correcting the mistake. Finding a mistake can be a great learning experience. The person who made the error will be far less likely to make the same error in the future. By using this correcting technique, you have not criticized the work but simply recognized that, like many space shuttle launches, delays are a part of exploration. Always place the emphasis on fixing the problem. You will thus reinforce the concept of risk taking and model the skill of problem solving.

3 Related Issues

Risk Taking

My teaching experience reminds me that creativity does not flourish without risk taking. As teachers, we must create an environment in which risk taking is encouraged and nurtured. We must teach it, yes, but we must also model it.

My mind looks back to the child in my classroom who was unwilling to raise a hand, a child who never volunteered yet who, I was convinced, was bright and capable. I'm sure we've all had students like this. The older our students, the more often this unwillingness to participate occurs.

One thing I loved about teaching kindergarten was the excitement and enthusiasm of the youngsters. Every day they came into my room with that look in their eyes that said, "What are we going to do today?" They couldn't wait to get started. Each day was an adventure. If I needed a volunteer, all I had to do was ask and almost every hand went up. Too many children start out loving school and end up holding their breath until graduation. Why?

Learning from Experience

Children learn from their experiences. They have raised their hands to volunteer and then regretted it. They have answered questions and known from the teacher's nonverbal response that they were wrong, and they were embarrassed. They have slipped down into their seats when a teacher has delighted in pointing out their shortcomings. Such experiences do not encourage children to become risk takers.

> **If we expect to increase the flow of creative ideas, we need to let students know that it is safe to take risks in our classrooms.**

As a result of uncomfortable, embarrassing, and negative experiences, many children will choose not to participate rather than to take a chance. They have learned their lesson from teachers and parents: If you don't know the correct answer, don't risk it. The price of failure is too great. No wonder creativity is stifled in classrooms today. The pores of invention have been clogged, and if we expect to increase the flow of creative ideas, we need to let students know that it is safe to take risks in our classrooms.

Of course, these experiences happen not only to students but to teachers, as well. Many school environments do not encourage teachers to experiment. The system often discourages diversity, variety, and innovation. Thus, rather than risk unknown consequences, we tend to conform. The environment in which we work can affect our own creative processes, which in turn can affect those of our students.

Model Risk Taking

One of the ways to demonstrate risk taking is to model it in your class. I recall an experience that illustrates how difficult such risks can be for some people. Several years ago I was a facilitator for a gifted program and I visited a teacher's room because I'd heard she was trying some unusual techniques. I waved as I tip-toed to the back of the room and took a seat so as not to disturb the class while the lesson was proceeding. Then I noticed the teacher slowly walking backward toward the chalkboard. As she continued without missing a beat, she wiped her elbow against the board to erase a misspelled word. The students watched but said nothing.

I was not there as an evaluator. I popped in only to pick up an idea or two. Yet despite the fact that this teacher knew me, she was very embarrassed by that misspelled word. Perhaps if she had known what a poor speller I was, she would not have reacted so strongly. But look at the nonverbal message she sent to her students. "It's not okay to make a mistake." "Errors are embarrassing."

Perfect teachers are a myth, but the myth is alive and well. Students seldom view teachers as making mistakes, yet to allow the myth of perfection to continue does not help the teacher-student relationship. We all know that some students look upon us as all-knowing, and some students even think that the teacher spends the night in the classroom. We are there when they arrive and we are there when they leave. For young children, it's a logical conclusion that we just pull out a little bed at night and roll it up during the day. If you have ever run into students in the grocery store, you know how shocked they can be that you eat food. What's more, if they see you wearing shorts they're amazed that you have knees.

If we show some vulnerability, however, we offer a connection that can be positive. If we make mistakes and survive them, we demonstrate a reality of life. We all make mistakes, and the important thing is that we learn from them. We don't often demonstrate this concept, and students have internalized the idea that mistakes are mortifying. And when children start to believe that they *are* mistakes, we have major self-esteem problems to overcome.

Problems Are Normal

In the world of work, problems are a part of everyday operations. Customer service departments have been created so that problems and mistakes can be corrected. Yet schools are perceived as places where blunders are the worst thing that can happen. We need to dwell more on the correcting of mistakes than on the making of them. Special effort should be made to separate the error from the person who made it. Society seems to enjoy the process of investigation to find the guilty party. Yet often the problem is forgotten once the culprit is discovered. This kind of thinking only condemns us to repeat history.

Think of your own situation for a moment. Suppose that you get a memo in your mailbox in the teacher's lounge. It refers to something that you can't figure out. Perhaps it has a deadline—it was due yesterday. You're frustrated, so what do you do? Would you go to the teacher who always has everything turned in on time? Would you go to the co-worker who is organized and always finishes report cards early? Probably you would go down the hall to another teacher who is frustrated and behind in his or her paperwork, also. You put your heads together and try to problem solve while deciphering the memo and planning a strategy for action.

If students look at their teachers as being perfect, they are less likely to come to those teachers with problems.

If students look at their teachers as being perfect, they are less likely to come to those teachers with problems. They may not even try to solve a problem for fear of being wrong. This may happen with parents as well. If your child thinks you don't make mistakes, or if you hide slip-ups from your children, you deprive them of the opportunity to learn that everyone can overcome mistakes. We can in fact learn from them and make better choices in the future. If we want children to come to us with problems, the children have to believe that we have experience in dealing with problems.

The environment that we create in the classroom and at home will send a message to our children. The message that "we all make mistakes here" tells children that they can fit in. By modeling we can demonstrate vividly what lectures can never accomplish.

Creative Mathematics

Looking to the future, we know there is not just one solution to the problems young people will have to solve. To prepare children for the future by allowing them to believe that the answer is either A, B, or C is to give them an illusion about problem solving. We cannot even imagine all the problems of the future, much less solve those problems. Students must be trained to think, to take chances, and even to risk disapproval from their peers if they are to become the inventors and creators of tomorrow.

Math can be creative. Providing activities that are divergent and yet convergent at the same time can encourage this creativity. Such exercises are often called "di-con" activities. The math loop is a di-con activity. The divergent part lies in discovering the many ways to get from one number to another. The convergent part is finding the one correct answer to the question. All the divergent paths must end up with the same convergent answer.

> **Students must be trained to think, to take chances, and even to risk disapproval from their peers if they are to become the inventors and creators of tomorrow.**

To demonstrate this di-con element to students, place a simple five-card loop diagram on the board, but use only the "I have" side of the diagram, allowing the "Who has" side to be blank. Let each student complete the loop by filling in the blank side of the diagram without discussing it with their classmates. The result will be as many different loops as you have students. Even though the "I have" part of each card will be the same, or convergent, the "Who has" part of the cards will be somewhat, or even completely, different. The model below shows how two students used the same convergent information to get two different loops. Even though the "I have" of each diagram is the same, the "Who has" columns are very different. The divergent aspect of the right column allows for, even encourages, creativity. With thirty kids in a class, you may end up with thirty different loops and yet all of them will be correct.

Student A

I Have	Who Has
8	this and 9 more?
17	this and 3 more + 2?
22	10 less than I do?
12	2 fewer than I have?
10	this + 6 divided by 2?

Student B

I Have	Who Has
8	double this plus 1?
17	5 more than this?
22	half of this + 1?
12	this + 8 divided by 2?
10	half of this + 3?

4

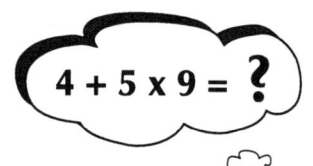

Mental Gymnastics

When I was in high school, I had a teacher who gave his class mental gymnastics every day, sometimes to start the class and sometimes to end it. What was involved was quite simple and yet it required students to listen and to perform mathematical calculations in their heads.

Here is an example of what you might say to demonstrate a mental math gymnastics activity: "I have four, plus five, times nine, minus one, divided by four, plus one, divided by seven, and the answer is?" Let a student volunteer to guess the answer. If students are following along, someone will know the answer is three. Sometimes a student will guess incorrectly. If this happens, ask if everyone agrees. If students argue, it might be necessary to do the problem on the board to verify the correct answer. The faster you present these gymnastics, the more exciting they can become.

Mental gymnastics can be a great sponge activity to start the class and get students warmed up.

This activity is multilevel. Whether you are teaching high school or elementary students, you should give students only the operations that they have mastered. The problem can be as complex or as simple as is appropriate.

When you are starting, it is good to allow everyone to feel successful. Try this one: "I'll start with two. Now double it, plus six, minus five. The answer is?" Someone will raise a hand and answer five.

After a couple of weeks of practicing mental gymnastics, ask for a student to volunteer to give one to the class. Mental gymnastics can be a great sponge activity to start the class and get students warmed up. The gymnastics get students' attention while sharpening their listening skills for the class period.

Some students will be better at this type of activity than others, and some will have difficulty listening and calculating at the same time. You might ask such a student to volunteer to write a gymnastic exercise for the next class period. After a year of daily mental gymnastics, students will be better listeners, and their facility with mental arithmetic operations may even surprise them.

5 Sample Math Loops

You can use the loops in this chapter to get started. Photocopy the pages, then cut apart the individual steps for each loop. You might then want to paste the steps on cards or simply use them as strips. If there are more cards than students, some students may hold two cards. The loops contain the following:

- Loop A. 24 cards. Numerals. Addition and subtraction.
- Loop B. 24 cards. Number words. Same as loop A plus multiplication.
- Loop C. 24 cards. Numerals and number words. Same as loop B plus division.
- Loop D. 24 cards. Numerals and number words. Same as loop C plus fractions.
- Loop E. 24 cards. Numerals and number words. Same as loop D plus squares, square roots, cubes, and cube roots.
- Loop F. 28 cards. Numerals and number words. Same as loop E plus algebra, geometry, and math terms.

Loop A: Addition and Subtraction

I have 10.

Who has 10 more than I do?

I have 4.

Who has 1 less than this?

I have 20.

Who has 10 more than I do?

I have 3.

Who has 1 less than this?

I have 30.

Who has this minus 30 plus 5?

I have 2.

Who has this minus 1?

I have 5.

Who has 1 less than this?

I have 1.

Who has 14 more than I do?

Loop A: Addition and Subtraction

I have 15.

Who has 10 more than this?

I have 12.

Who has this minus 2, plus 4?

I have 25.

Who has 4 less than I do?

I have 14.

Who has one less than I do?

I have 21.

Who has this minus 3?

I have 13.

Who has this minus 3, plus 1?

I have 18.

Who has this minus 4, minus 2 more?

I have 11.

Who has 2 less than this?

Loop A: Addition and Subtraction

I have 9. *Who has 3 less than I do?*	**I have 16.** *Who has this minus 6, plus 9?*
I have 6. *Who has 1 more than this?*	**I have 19.** *Who has 3 more than this?*
I have 7. *Who has this and 1 more?*	**I have 22.** *Who has this minus 2, plus 4?*
I have 8. *Who has this and 8 more?*	**I have 24.** *Who has this minus 4, minus 10?*

Loop B: Addition, Subtraction, and Multiplication

I have two.

Who has this times four?

I have twelve.

Who has this plus four?

I have eight.

Who has this minus three?

I have sixteen.

Who has this minus one, plus five?

I have five.

Who has this times two, minus one?

I have twenty.

Who has five more than this?

I have nine.

Who has this minus three, times two?

I have twenty-five.

Who has this times two?

Loop B: Addition, Subtraction, and Multiplication

I have fifty.

Who has fifty less than this plus one?

I have six.

Who has this times two, minus one.

I have one.

Who has this times three?

I have eleven.

Who has this minus one?

I have three.

Who has one more than I do?

I have ten.

Who has this minus five, times three?

I have four.

Who has this minus one, times two?

I have fifteen.

Who has this minus ten, times six?

Loop B: Addition, Subtraction, and Multiplication

I have thirty.

Who has this minus thirty plus seven?

I have twenty-one.

Who has one less than this, times two, plus two?

I have seven.

Who has six more than this?

I have forty-two.

Who has two less than this, plus ten, times two?

I have thirteen.

Who has this minus six, times two?

I have one hundred.

Who has this minus one hundred, plus forty.

I have fourteen.

Who has this minus seven, times three?

I have forty.

Who has this minus forty, plus two.

Loop C: Addition, Subtraction, Multiplication, and Division

I have 10.

Who has this divided by 2?

I have 100.

Who has 90 less than this, plus 2?

I have 5.

Who has this times 5?

I have 12.

Who has this minus six, times six?

I have 25.

Who has double this?

I have 36.

Who has this minus one, divided by 5?

I have 50.

Who has twice as much as I do?

I have 7.

Who has this times seven?

Loop C: Addition, Subtraction, Multiplication, and Division

I have 49.

Who has two more than this?

I have 16.

Who has this minus 9, times 3?

I have 51.

Who has this minus one, divided by two, minus one?

I have 21.

Who has this minus 3, divided by 3?

I have 24.

Who has this divided by 6?

I have 6.

Who has this number times 6, plus 6?

I have 4.

Who has this number times itself?

I have 42.

Who has this divided by 2, minus 6?

Loop C: Addition, Subtraction, Multiplication, and Division

I have 15.

Who has this divided by 5, times 10?

I have 1,634,675.

Who has this times 0?

I have 30.

Who has this times 2, plus 4, divided by 8?

I have 0.

Who has this plus 500?

I have 8.

Who has this divided by 8?

I have 500.

Who has this times 2?

I have 1.

Who has this times 1,634,675?

I have 1000.

Who has this divided by 100?

Loop D: Includes Fractions

I have 4.

Who has half of this?

I have 50.

Who has one-tenth of this?

I have 2.

Who has this times 6?

I have 5.

Who has this times itself?

I have 12.

Who has one-half of this times 8?

I have 25.

Who has double this, plus 50?

I have 48.

Who has this plus 2?

I have 100.

Who has one-tenth of this?

Loop D: Includes Fractions

I have 10. *Who has this times 100?*	**I have 75.** *Who has one-third of this, plus 2?*
I have 1,000. *Who has half of this?*	**I have 27.** *Who has one-ninth of this?*
I have 500. *Who has this minus 200?*	**I have 3.** *Who has this times 432, divided by 2, minus 0, times 0.*
I have 300. *Who has one-third of this, minus 25?*	**I have zero.** *Who has this plus 49?*

Think Math! © 1995 Zephyr Press, Tucson, AZ

Loop D: Includes Fractions

I have 49.

Who has one-seventh of this?

I have 36.

Who has one-sixth of this?

I have 7.

Who has this times 3?

I have 6.

Who has this times 100, divided by 2, divided by 2 again?

I have 21.

Who has one-third of this times 5?

I have 150.

Who has this divided by 150?

I have 35.

Who has this plus 1?

I have 1.

Who has this plus 15, divided by 4?

42 Think Math! © 1995 Zephyr Press, Tucson, AZ

Loop E: Includes Squares, Square Roots, Cubes, and Cube Roots

I have 3. *Who has the square of this?*	**I have 16.** *Who has the square root of this plus 1?*
I have 9. *Who has this times 2?*	**I have 5.** *Who has this number squared?*
I have 18. *Who has this plus 2?*	**I have 25.** *Who has this times 4?*
I have 20. *Who has one-fifth of this squared?*	**I have 100.** *Who has half of this, plus 31?*

Think Math! © 1995 Zephyr Press, Tucson, AZ

Loop E: Includes Squares, Square Roots, Cubes, and Cube Roots

I have 81.

Who has the square root of this, plus 2?

I have 200.

Who has half of this, divided by 2, minus 1?

I have 11.

Who has three less than I do?

I have 49.

Who has the square root of this, plus 3?

I have 8.

Who has the cube root of this?

I have 10.

Who has triple this, plus 6?

I have 2.

Who has this times 100?

I have 36.

Who has the square root of this?

Loop E: Includes Squares, Square Roots, Cubes, and Cube Roots

I have 6. *Who has one-sixth of this, times 1.2 million?*	**I have 12.** *Who has this squared?*
I have 1.2 million. *Who has this divided by 0?*	**I have 144.** *Who has this plus 6, divided by 50, plus 10?*
I have zero. *Who has this plus 64?*	**I have 13.** *Who has this plus 7, divided by 5?*
I have 64. *Who has the square root of this, plus 4?*	**I have 4.** *Who has this squared, minus 13?*

Think Math! © 1995 Zephyr Press, Tucson, AZ

Loop F: Includes Algebra, Geometry, and Math Terms

I have equation.

Who has the symbol that shows equality?

I have = (equals sign).

Who has a times a?

I have a^2.

Who has 4a times b?

I have 4ab.

Who has 3b minus b?

I have 2b.

Who has b times b^2?

I have b^3.

Who has the name of the 3 in b^3?

I have exponent.

Who has the term for arithmetical mean of several numbers?

I have average.

Who has the term for shortest distance between two points?

Loop F: Includes Algebra, Geometry, and Math Terms

I have line.

Who has the term for one-360th of a circle?

I have equilateral triangle.

Who has the number of degrees in each of my angles?

I have one degree.

Who has the number of degrees in a right angle?

I have 60°.

Who has the name of an angle that is greater than 90?

I have 90°.

Who has the name of an angle that has fewer degrees than I have?

I have obtuse angle.

Who has a four-sided figure with opposite sides parallel?

I have acute.

Who has the name of a triangle with 3 equal sides?

I have parallelogram.

Who has a six-sided figure?

Loop F: Includes Algebra, Geometry, and Math Terms

I have hexagon. *Who has the name of the answer to an addition problem?*	**I have octagon.** *Who has the name of the answer to a subtraction problem?*
I have sum. *Who has the name of the answer to a multiplication problem?*	**I have difference.** *Who has a mixed number?*
I have product. *Who has the number of sides of a triangle?*	**I have $3\frac{1}{2}$.** *Who has the name for the bottom number in a fraction?*
I have 3. *Who has the name of an 8-sided figure?*	**I have denominator.** *Who has the name for the top number in a fraction?*

Loop F: Includes Algebra, Geometry, and Math Terms

I have numerator.

Who has the name for the point where two lines cross?

I have quadrilateral.

Who has the name for the side of a triangle that is opposite a right angle?

I have intersection.

Who has a figure with four right angles?

I have hypotenuse.

Who has the expression of equality between two operations?

Think Math! © 1995 Zephyr Press, Tucson, AZ

6
Sample Loops for Language Arts

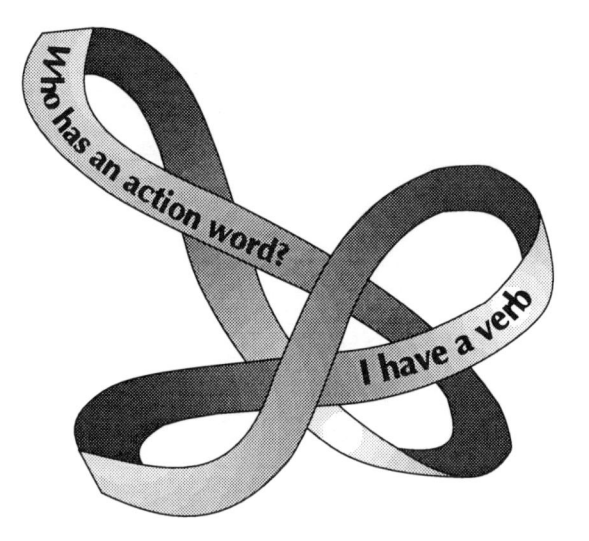

This chapter contains two sample language arts loops. Again, you can photocopy the pages, cut the strips apart, paste the strips onto cards, and distribute cards to students. Loops contain the following:

▶ Loop A. 24 cards. Definitions of parts of speech, grammar, punctuation, and so on.

▶ Loop B. 22 cards. Synonyms and antonyms.

Loop A: Parts of Speech, Grammar, and Punctuation

I have a noun. *Who has an action word?*	**I have a declarative sentence.** *Who has a sentence that gives a command?*
I have a verb. *Who has a word that modifies a verb?*	**I have an imperative sentence.** *Who has a sentence that asks a question?*
I have an adverb. *Who has something that sets off a person's exact words?*	**I have an interrogative sentence.** *Who has a sentence that expresses strong feelings?*
I have quotation marks. *Who has a sentence that makes a statement?*	**I have an exclamatory sentence.** *Who has a sentence that is made up of two or more independent clauses and no subordinate clauses?*

Think Math! © 1995 Zephyr Press, Tucson, AZ

Loop A: Parts of Speech, Grammar, and Punctuation

I have a compound sentence. *Who has a word that can take the place of a noun?*	**I have an antonym.** *Who has the punctuation mark that is found at the end of a declarative sentence?*
I have a pronoun. *Who has a word that joins words or groups of words?*	**I have a period.** *Who has the punctuation mark that is found at the end of an interrogative sentence?*
I have a conjunction. *Who has a word whose meaning is the same or similar to another word?*	**I have a question mark.** *Who has the type of letter that always begins a sentence?*
I have a synonym. *Who has a word whose meaning is the opposite of another word?*	**I have a capital letter.** *Who has a mark that takes the place of a missing letter or letters in a contraction?*

Loop A: Parts of Speech, Grammar, and Punctuation

I have an apostrophe. *Who has the part of a letter with the written name of the person sending the letter?*	**I have an adjective.** *Who has two words put together to make one word?*
I have the signature. *Who has the part of a letter near the end that says "Sincerely" or "Yours truly?"*	**I have a compound word.** *What word describes all letters of the alphabet except* a, e, i, o, u, *and sometimes* y?
I have the closing. *Who has the main part of a letter?*	**I have consonants.** *Who has all the other letters in the alphabet?*
I have the body of a letter. *Who has a word that modifies a noun?*	**I have vowels.** *Who has a person, place, or thing?*

Loop B: Synonyms and Antonyms

I have sharp.

Who has a synonym of happy?

I have thin.

Who has a synonym of friend?

I have joyful.

Who has an antonym of ugly?

I have chum.

Who has an antonym of old?

I have beautiful.

Who has a synonym of short?

I have young.

Who has a synonym of big?

I have brief.

Who has an antonym of fat?

I have large.

Who has an antonym of evil?

Loop B: Synonyms and Antonyms

I have good.

Who has a synonym of very old?

I have crooked.

Who has a synonym of footwear?

I have ancient.

Who has an antonym of weak?

I have shoe.

Who has an antonym of empty?

I have strong.

Who has a synonym of girl?

I have full.

Who has a synonym of city?

I have female.

Who has an antonym of straight?

I have town.

Who has an antonym of left?

Loop B: Synonyms and Antonyms

I have right.

Who has a synonym of teacher?

I have pupil.

Who has an antonym of tough?

I have instructor.

Who has an antonym of dark?

I have tender.

Who has a synonym of chew?

I have light.

Who has a synonym of student?

I have gnaw.

Who has an antonym of dull?

7
Sample Social Studies Loop

This chapter contains a sample social studies loop. Again, you can photocopy the pages, cut the strips apart, paste the strips onto cards, and distribute cards to students. The loop contains ten cards with a variety of social studies questions covering several topics.

Sample Social Studies Loop

I have North America.

Who has the largest continent on Earth?

I have Asia.

Who has the smallest continent?

I have Antarctica.

Who has the year that the American War between the States began?

I have 1861.

Who has the leader of the southern army during the Civil War?

I have Robert E. Lee.

Who has the American president during the Civil War?

I have Abraham Lincoln.

Who has the name of the state in which he was born?

I have Kentucky.

Who has the name of the U.S. state that was first bombed by the Japanese in 1941?

I have Hawai'i.

Who has the president that led America into World War II?

Sample Social Studies Loop

I have Franklin D. Roosevelt.

Who has the name of his plan to end the Great Depression?

I have the New Deal.

Who has the continent on which the United States is located?

8 Sample Science Loop

This chapter contains a sample science loop. Again, you can photocopy the pages, cut the strips apart, paste the strips onto cards, and distribute cards to students. The loop contains ten cards with a variety of science questions covering several scientific disciplines.

Sample Science Loop

I have antennae. *Who has the name of the body part of an insect on which these are located?*	**I have eight.** *Who has the type of multi-faceted vision used by most insects?*
I have head. *Who has the part of the body of an insect where the legs are attached?*	**I have compound eye.** *Who has an insect known for jumping?*
I have thorax. *Who has the number of legs that an insect has?*	**I have grasshopper.** *Who has an insect that can make a lot of noise at night?*
I have six. *Who has the number of legs that a spider has?*	**I have cricket.** *Who has the name of an insect's cocoon?*

Think Math! © 1995 Zephyr Press, Tucson, AZ

Sample Science Loop

I have chrysalis.

Who has the stage of an insect when it eats the most?

I have larva.

Who has the name for an insect's feelers?

9
Sample Loop for Multiple Content Areas

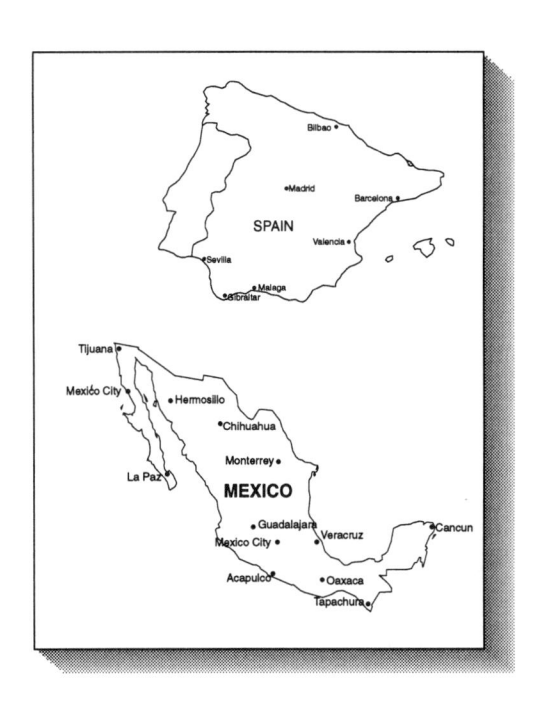

For a student to transfer knowledge from one subject area to another is a sign of a thinking mind. For teachers of self-contained classrooms, this is not a new concept. The following loop adapts itself very well to multiple parts of the curriculum. Here is a sample to play with and help get a class started.

Again, you can photocopy the pages, cut the strips apart, paste the strips onto cards, and distribute cards to students. The loop contains fourteen cards with a variety of questions covering several disciplines.

Sample Loop for Multiple Content Areas

I have 4.

Who has half of this?

I have yellow.

Who has the closest star to Earth that is the same color as I am?

I have 2.

Who has one more than I do?

I have the sun.

Who has the planet closest to it?

I have three.

Who has the color of yellow and blue mixed together?

I have Mercury.

Who has the temperature at which water boils on a Celsius thermometer?

I have green.

Who has orange minus red?

I have 100.

Who has the capital of Texas?

Sample Loop for Multiple Content Areas

I have Austin.

Who has the capital of Ohio?

I have Mexico.

Who has the number of states in the United States?

I have Columbus.

Who has the country that he sailed from in 1492?

I have 50.

Who has this minus 50?

I have Spain.

Who has the country in North America that Columbus was given credit for colonizing?

I have zero.

Who has four more than I do?

Think Math! © 1995 Zephyr Press, Tucson, AZ

10 Sample Problem Solving Activities

This section of the book includes activities not related to loops. They are activities I have used over the years to stimulate interest in and practice of problem solving while having fun. These activities encourage risk taking, foster deductive reasoning, and are at the same time enjoyable for students.

How Tall Is the School?

"How tall is our school?" asks the teacher. No one knows the answer. The logical way to find out is to measure it, but visions of students on ladders with other students on their shoulders triggers images of lawsuits and front page headlines: "Three Children Injured as Teacher Risks Their Lives to Make a Point!"

Children have always been fascinated with big or tall things, so use this natural curiosity to help children learn how to measure things that nobody can reach, including anything that touches the ground, such as trees, flag poles, tall buildings, and gymnasiums. As long as there is an open area between the base of the structure to be measured and the end of the shadow it casts, almost anything can be measured.

Before you begin, you might have students brainstorm ways to measure the height of the school without using a ladder or scaling the wall. You may get some very creative answers, some of which might be practical and some not. Perhaps someone will come up with the method presented in this chapter, which is easy and practical.

Once you decide on the object to be measured, let students determine the length of the shadow (from the base of the object to the end of the shadow). Encourage students to do their measuring in meters or centimeters, since it is good to get practice in using metrics. If the shadow is too long to get a clear measurement, wait until a different time of the day when the shadow is shorter or cast in a different direction.

Next, have a student hold a meter stick on its end, where the shadow of the structure ends. Then have another student measure the length of the shadow cast by the meter stick. Now you have three bits of data: the length of the meter stick, the length of the meter stick's shadow, and the length of the shadow cast by the structure.

By setting up a simple equation to determine proportion, you can easily find the height of the structure, as shown below:

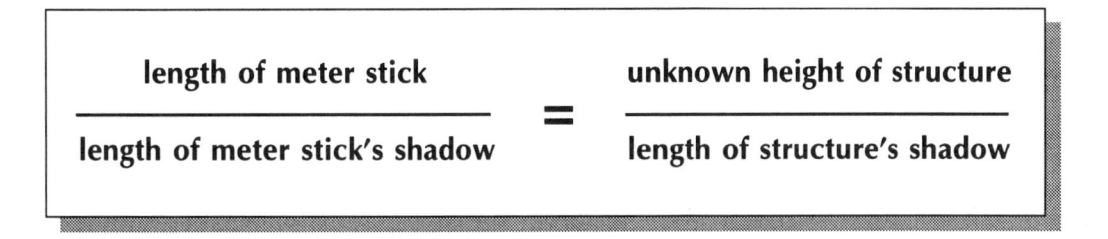

$$\frac{\text{length of meter stick}}{\text{length of meter stick's shadow}} = \frac{\text{unknown height of structure}}{\text{length of structure's shadow}}$$

Suppose the following were the measurements: The meter stick is 100 centimeters, the meter stick casts a shadow of 32.5 centimeters, and the shadow of the structure is 788 centimeters. By placing this information into an equation to determine proportion, your students can easily determine the unknown height without climbing the structure.

$$\frac{100 \text{ centimeters}}{32.5 \text{ centimeters}} = \frac{\text{unknown or X}}{788 \text{ centimeters}}$$

Students can solve the equation by cross multiplying: 100 centimeters times 788 centimeters will equal x times 32.5 centimeters or:

$$X \times 32.5 = 78800 \text{ cm.}$$

Next divide both sides of the equation by 32.5 to discover the value of x. The result is x = 2424.6153 cm. Therefore the height of the unknown structure is a little over 2,424 centimeters, or approximately 24 meters high. That's more than 72 feet high—too tall for students to climb and measure.

Students can also establish a ratio between the shadows and the objects that is the same for both objects. For example, the ratio of the meter stick to its shadow is approximately one to three. This means that the shadow is about one-third the length of the stick. Therefore the shadow of the building (or other object to be measured) will be about one-third of its actual height. The ratio will change depending on the time of day, but the relationship between the stick's ratio and the building's ratio will remain constant. No matter what time of the day the measuring takes place, as long as both shadows are measured at the same time, the proportion will be the same and height of the structure will stay the same.

Try it! Your students will like it! You'll like it!

Building a Scale Model of the Solar System

The enormous distances in space are very difficult for youngsters—or anyone—to comprehend. The concept of light traveling at 186,000 miles per second can be hard even for adults to grasp. Observers of a sunrise may not realize that the sun actually cleared the horizon eight minutes earlier. Because of the distance from Earth to its sun, approximately 93,000,000 miles, it has taken the light that long to get to the spot of the observers. Such concepts can be mind boggling, but we owe it to our students to help them understand the world in which they live—and that includes the universe!

The best way to help students understand the massive size of our solar system is to let them make a scale model—not a model but a scale model. Students have seen models of the solar system and usually their perception is that the planets are revolving around the sun in concentric orbits about equidistant from each other. Yet nothing could be further from the truth.

Before students begin their calculations, find the longest hall in the school building and measure its length in meters and centimeters. This measurement will determine the scale your students will use. One end of the hall will represent the sun's location and the other end will be Pluto's orbit.

Suppose the distance is about 120 feet; that's about 37 meters or 3,700 centimeters. Since Pluto is more than $3\frac{1}{2}$ billion miles from the sun, that would make each centimeter in the hallway equal to about 1 million miles. If you want to round it off to a million miles, no problem. This model is not going to be exactly to scale.

Once you set the scale for distance, let students do the calculations. With these types of distances you may want to let them practice exponents; one centimeter is equal to 1×10^6 miles. Following are the approximate distances of each planet from the sun.

Mercury	=	35,960,000	miles or	36×10^6
Venus	=	67,000,000	miles or	67×10^6
Earth	=	93,000,000	miles or	93×10^6
Mars	=	141,600,000	miles or	142×10^6
Jupiter	=	483,000,000	miles or	483×10^6
Saturn	=	886,000,000	miles or	886×10^6
Uranus	=	1,783,000,000	miles or	1783×10^6
Neptune	=	2,794,000,000	miles or	2794×10^6
Pluto	=	3,670,000,000	miles or	3670×10^6

For the scale used, the distances in centimeters would be approximately

Mercury	=	36 centimeters
Venus	=	67 centimeters
Earth	=	93 centimeters
Mars	=	142 centimeters
Jupiter	=	483 centimeters
Saturn	=	886 centimeters
Uranus	=	1,783 centimeters
Neptune	=	2,794 centimeters
Pluto	=	3,670 centimeters

Sample Problem Solving Activities

When students mark off the hallway floor or wall with tape, they are ready to hang the planets from the ceiling. If you decide to do the size of the planets by scale, a different ratio than the one used for distances will be necessary because the sun is huge compared to the planets. Since the sun's diameter is about 865,000 miles and the Earth's diameter is only about 8,000 miles, the ratio is more than 100 to 1. Thus, if Earth is only 1 centimeter in diameter, the Sun will be more than 100 centimeters. The problem comes when trying to make the Earth's moon, whose diameter is about one-fourth of the Earth's. That means the moon will be so small that its label will cover it up. The moons from other planets will then become about pinhead size or less.

Another method you can use is to let a very large arc on the wall represent the sun; then make the other planets to scale. Start with Jupiter, the largest. You don't want it to hang down too low in the hall or students will bang into it when they are changing classes.

Once students see this graphic representation, they will better understand why life as we know it is more likely to occur on Earth than on the more distant planets in our solar system. The location of the asteroid belt may stimulate discussion of the possibility of an ancient planet or something that exploded long ago. Allow plenty of time for this project!

Horses and Zebras

This activity is great for the backseat of the car, and it also works well in the classroom. It is designed to let students have fun with place value while they put number digits in the correct place through the use of deductive reasoning. The only materials needed are paper and pencils. Players may be in teams of two or three. Two is best because it offers the most opportunity to respond and the game moves faster.

The first rule is to know the difference between a horse and a zebra. A horse is a correct digit in the correct place. A zebra is a correct digit in the wrong place. The "leader" thinks of a two-digit number. The "player" tries to discover that number in as few guesses as possible. The leader's responses to the guesses will give clues as to whether the number has one of the correct digits and, if so, whether it is in the correct place. The leader will respond to the guesses because she or he knows the answer.

For example, what if the leader is thinking of the number 46 and the other player guesses 12? The leader would respond, "That has zero horses and zero zebras." The player would then know that the digits one and two do not appear in the number the leader has chosen. Suppose the player then guesses the number 34. The leader would then answer, "That has zero horses and one zebra." That response tells the player that one of the digits is correct but is in the wrong place and that the other digit doesn't appear at all. At this point the player is not sure which number is correct and which one is not. Perhaps the player now guesses 76. The leader would answer, "That has one horse and zero zebras." This tells the player that one of the digits is correct and in the correct place. The player still does not know which number is correct and which one does not appear at all. Many of the choices have now been reduced, however, and the clever player will work with combinations until the correct one is discovered.

Perhaps the leader is thinking of the number 14. Following are the correct responses to certain guesses:

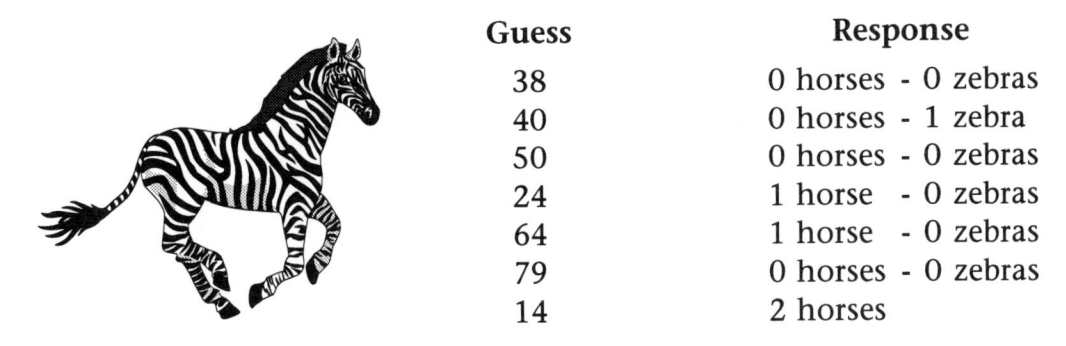

Guess	Response
38	0 horses - 0 zebras
40	0 horses - 1 zebra
50	0 horses - 0 zebras
24	1 horse - 0 zebras
64	1 horse - 0 zebras
79	0 horses - 0 zebras
14	2 horses

The responses give clues that help the player eliminate certain numbers. By carefully choosing numbers based on the leader's responses, the player will sharpen those skills of deductive reasoning.

To begin the game, let one of the team members be the leader and the other the player. When the player has guessed the number, the leader and the player switch roles and start again. The goal is to derive the answer in as few guesses as possible. If students are playing the game competitively, have them keep a tabulation of the number of guesses each player makes in each round. After each member has played several times, let each person add up the total number of guesses. The one with the lowest total wins that series of games.

Students will probably develop strategies as they practice. Some will keep track of their guesses on paper and others will remember them. In my experience, the player sometimes accuses the leader of changing the number, so leaders might want to record the correct number in a hidden place so that it can be validated later.

When two-digit numbers are mastered, encourage students to go on to three-digit and even four-digit numbers. These numbers are more challenging, but the larger number of possibilities makes them more interesting. In my experience, it is best to ask beginning students not to use double digits (55, 77, 99, and so on). For example, what if the correct number is 88, and the player guesses 18? Technically the 8 is a zebra as well as a horse. The 8 is in the correct place for the 8 in the ones place, but in the wrong place for the 8 in the tens place. This can cause confusion until clear strategies are developed through practice.

How Did It Do That?

Curiosity is one of the greatest motivators of children, yet too often we begin lessons by telling students what they are going to do and how they are going to do it. Discovery lessons are different. They allow the students to become risk takers because you do not tell them everything ahead of time. Instead, you expose them to an idea or activity and then ask them to problem solve in order to discover why something happens. Problem solving is why hypothesizing is so much fun, and yet it is a technique that is seldom used.

Here are several math puzzles that will cause students to ask, "How did you do that?" When they ask that type of question, they are hooked. Allow different students to discover different methods. There may be more than one way to explain or solve a problem. The fun is in the fact that the problems are self-correcting. Students will know if they have made an error, and if so, they can go back and try to discover the mistake. This game is a great way to practice arithmetic operations. It is also a great calculator activity.

Problem 1

Tell your students to choose a number, any number. Then tell them, "Don't let anyone see it. Now take that number and add three to it. When you get your answer, multiply it by two. Take this number and subtract four. Now divide the answer by two. After dividing, subtract your original number—the number you started out with." The answer will be one. Every student in the class should have the answer one unless someone made a calculation error. Now ask the class why this is so.

> Try a sample number, 13.
>
> Now add 3. That gives 16.
>
> Next multiply by 2. The product is 32.
>
> Next, subtract 4, which gives 28.
>
> Now divide by 2 and the quotient will be 14.
>
> By subtracting the original number 13, the answer will be 1.
>
> Students will have fun explaining why this works every time.

Problem 2

Again, pick a number, any number (say you choose 4). Now add the next larger number to it (that is, add 5). After obtaining this sum, add 9 to it. Then divide the result by 2 and subtract the original number. The answer is 5. Why?

    Start with the number 8.

    Add the next larger number, 9, and the answer is 17.

    Now add 9 to this and you get 26.

    Divide this by 2 and you get 13.

    Now subtract the original number, 8, and the answer is 5, which is the correct answer.

Problem 3

This trick allows you to determine the age of each student in the class as well as the amount of loose change in students' pockets, if it is less than a dollar.

Begin by asking students to take a piece of paper and write down their age so that you cannot see it. They will next multiply that number by 4. After they have an answer, they should add 10. Now have them multiply the answer by 25. Now they should subtract the number of days in a year (365). Next tell students to add the change that they are carrying if it is less than one dollar. If they have no change they can make up a fictitious amount. Do not use the decimal point. After students have an answer, they should add 115. Each student will now have a four-digit number. The thousands and hundreds digits will be equal to their ages, and the tens and ones digits will be the change less than a dollar.

    For example, start with the age of 16.

    Multiply this amount by 4. This gives the answer 64.

    Now add 10, and the result is 74.

    Next multiply 74 by 25; the product is 1850.

    By subtracting the number of days in a year, or 365, you get 1485.

    Suppose this student has 38 cents in his pocket.

    Add 38 to 1485 and you get 1523.

    Finally, add 115 to 1523 and the answer is 1638.

    Therefore, the student is 16 years old and has 38 cents.

Sample Problem Solving Activities

Problem 4

This problem will work with students ages 10 and older who have fewer than 10 people in their family. First have students multiply their age by 2. Now add 10. Multiply this sum by 5 and then add the number of people in the family. Finally, subtract 50. The age will appear in the hundreds and tens places, and the number of family members appears in the ones place.

> For example, begin with the age of 12.
>
> Multiply it by 2 and the answer is 24.
>
> Now add 10 and the result is 34.
>
> Multiply this number by 5 and the product is 170.
>
> If there are 7 members in the family, add 7 to 170 and the sum is 177.
>
> Then subtract 50; the final answer is 127.
>
> From this you can tell that the person is 12 years old and has 7 family members.

Problem 5

Have students double their house numbers. Next add the number of days in a week. Multiply the result by 50 and add one's age. Now subtract the number of days in a year and add 15. The tens and ones digits equal the person's age, and the rest of the number is the house number.

If a 15-year-old lives at a street address of 1205, the problem would look like this:

> Double the house number, which results in 2,410.
>
> Add 7 (days in a week) and you get 2,417.
>
> Multiply 2,417 by 50 and the answer is 120,850.
>
> Add 15 (the age) to get 120,865.
>
> By subtracting the number of days in a year you get 120,500.
>
> Finally, add 15 to arrive at 120,515.
>
> The units and tens digits give the age and the rest is the house number.

The Magic of Nine

Take any row of digits making up a number and reverse them. After reversing the order, place the larger number on top and subtract the smaller one to get the difference. Add together all the digits in the answer. Next add all the digits in that answer. Continue this process until you end up with a single digit. That digit will always be nine. Follow the samples below.

Start with a number such as 57,281,905.

Now reverse the numbers and you will get 50,918,275.

Put the larger one on top and subtract the smaller one from it, and you will get a difference of 6,363,630.

Add these digits: 6 + 3 + 6 + 3 + 6 + 3 + 0 = 27.

Again, add the digits in the answer: 2 + 7 = 9.

Let's try another number. Start with 793,411.

Reverse it to make 114,397.

Subtract the smaller number and the difference is 679,014.

Add these digits and you will find: 6 + 7 + 9 + 0 + 1 + 4 = 27.

Again, add the digits in the answer: 2 + 7 = 9.

This process will work with any number, even very large ones.

Try a long number. Start with 893,476,598,234,565.

Reverse it to make 565,432,895,674,398.

Subtract them and the difference is 328,043,702,560,167.

Add these digits and you will find:
3 + 2 + 8 + 0 + 4 + 3 + 7 + 0 + 2 + 5 + 6 + 0 + 1 + 6 + 7 = 54.

Again, add the digits in the answer: 5 + 4 = 9.

What a great way to practice addition and subtraction. Every problem is self-correcting because the answer has to be nine. If not, try to discover the error.

Sample Problem Solving Activities

Magic Number Squares

Magic Squares are an easy way for students to make and work puzzles that require problem solving, discovery of patterns, and the practicing of addition. Place the numerals 1, 2, 3, 4, 5, 6, 7, 8, and 9 in three columns of three. There are several ways to arrange the numbers so that, when added vertically, horizontally, and diagonally, the answer will always be 15. Look at the following figure:

8	3	4
1	5	9
6	7	2

Notice that no matter which way they are added, the three numbers in a row always total 15. Are there any other possible arrangements? Yes. See the following example.

6	1	8
7	5	3
2	9	4

There are other ways to arrange the numbers, but allow students to discover a pattern. This magic square will work with any nine numbers in sequence. The sum will be different depending on the numbers used, but the sum in all three directions will be the same. For example try 25, 26, 27, 28, 29, 30, 31, 32, 33. Once students discover the pattern, they can amaze anyone who hasn't found the secret.

The pattern works also with four-by-four magic squares. The example below uses 1, 2, 3, 4, 5, 6, 7, 8, 9, 10, 11, 12, 13, 14, 15, and 16:

16	3	2	13
5	10	11	8
9	6	7	12
4	15	14	1

No matter which direction the numbers are added, the sum is 34. As long as the numbers used are in sequential order, the magic squares will work with five numbers across by five down, six numbers across by six down, seven numbers across by seven down, and so on. What an interesting way to play with and discover patterns while practicing arithmetic.

11
Math Loops for Grade Four

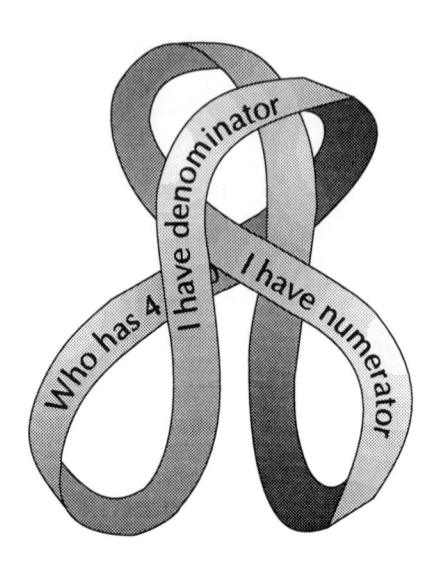

The loops in this chapter and the following chapters are not meant to be an accurate list of math skills by grade level for all schools. The math concepts I have used are those most often mentioned for each grade level in Texas's "essential elements." Please use these loops only as a guide or suggestion, not a curriculum outline. Modify and adapt to your own students' abilities, skills, interests, and needs.

Sample Loop A for Grade Four

I have numerator.

Who has the name of the bottom part of a fraction?

I have an odd number.

Who has four multiplied by ten?

I have denominator.

Who has a fraction that is equivalent to five-tenths?

I have forty.

Who has four multiplied by one hundred?

I have one-half.

Who has the name of a number that can be divided evenly by two?

I have four hundred.

Who has four multiplied by one thousand?

I have an even number.

Who has a number that cannot be divided evenly?

I have four thousand.

Who has four multiplied by ten thousand?

Sample Loop A for Grade Four

I have forty thousand.

Who has the answer to a division problem?

I have fifteen cents.

Who has the way to find the area of a rectangle?

I have quotient.

Who has what is left over after a division problem is finished?

I have length times width.

Who has the area of a square that has a side measuring eight inches?

I have remainder.

Who has the amount of change due from a dollar after a seventy-five-cent purchase?

I have sixty-four square inches.

Who has the area of a rectangle that has sides measuring four feet, four feet, eight feet, and eight feet?

I have twenty-five cents.

Who has the amount of change due from a dollar after an eighty-five-cent purchase?

I have thirty-two square feet.

Who has the numerator of the fraction one-half?

Think Math! © 1995 Zephyr Press, Tucson, AZ

Sample Loop A for Grade Four

I have one.

Who has the denominator of the fraction three-fourths?

I have four.

Who has a fractional equivalent of one-third?

I have two-sixths.

Who has a fractional equivalent of two-thirds?

I have four-sixths.

Who has eight times one thousand?

I have eight thousand.

Who has eight times one hundred?

I have eight hundred.

Who has eight times ten?

I have eighty.

Who has eight times ten thousand?

I have eighty thousand.

Who has the name for the top part of a fraction?

Think Math! © 1995 Zephyr Press, Tucson, AZ

Sample Loop B for Grade Four

I have a quadrilateral. *Who has the length of one side of a square with an area of eighty-one square feet?*	**I have forty-nine square meters.** *Who has the amount equal to my four quarters?*
I have nine feet. *Who has the length of one side of a square with an area of eighty-one square inches?*	**I have one dollar.** *Who has seventy-five cents less than I do?*
I have nine inches. *Who has the area of a square that has one side measuring seven feet in length?*	**I have twenty-five cents.** *Who has twice as much as I have?*
I have forty-nine square feet. *Who has the area of a square that has one side measuring seven meters in length?*	**I have half a dollar.** *Who has three times as much as I do?*

Sample Loop B for Grade Four

I have one dollar and fifty cents. *Who has the equivalent of ten pennies?*	**I have one dollar and twenty-five cents.** *Who has a word that describes two lines that are always the same distance apart?*
I have a dime. *Who has an amount equal to twenty dimes?*	**I have parallel lines.** *Who has the word for a line that is straight across from left to right or right to left?*
I have two dollars. *Who has change from a five-dollar bill after buying two dollars and fifty cents worth of candy?*	**I have horizontal line.** *Who has a word for a line that is straight up and down?*
I have two dollars and fifty cents. *Who has half of what I have?*	**I have vertical line.** *Who has the name for lines that go straight up and down from a horizontal line?*

Think Math! © 1995 Zephyr Press, Tucson, AZ

Sample Loop B for Grade Four

I have perpendicular lines. *Who has the name for a three-dimensional shape that is round at the bottom and goes up to a point at the top?*	**I have a cube.** *Who has a three-dimensional shape that is long and is circular at both ends?*
I have a cone. *Who has the name for a three-dimensional shape that is a square at the bottom and goes up to a point at the top?*	**I have a cylinder.** *Who has the Celsius temperature at which water freezes?*
I have a pyramid. *Who has a three-dimensional shape that is completely round?*	**I have zero degrees.** *Who has the Fahrenheit temperature at which water freezes?*
I have a sphere. *Who has a three-dimensional shape that is perfectly square in every direction?*	**I have thirty-two degrees.** *Who has the name for a four-sided, two-dimensional figure?*

Sample Loop C for Grade Four

I have one hundred degrees.

Who has the Fahrenheit temperature at which water boils?

I have sixteen.

Who has the number of quarts in a gallon?

I have two hundred twelve degrees.

Who has one-fourth of a gallon?

I have four.

Who has the number of centimeters in a meter?

I have one quart.

Who has one-fourth of this?

I have one hundred.

Who has the number of meters in a kilometer?

I have one cup.

Who has the number of cups in a gallon?

I have one thousand.

Who has the number of inches in a foot?

Sample Loop C for Grade Four

I have twelve. *Who has the number of inches in a yard?*	**I have sixteen.** *Who has the number of pounds in a ton?*
I have thirty-six. *Who has the number of feet in a yard?*	**I have two thousand.** *Who has the number of pints in a quart?*
I have three. *Who has the number of feet in a mile?*	**I have two.** *Who has the number of minutes in half an hour?*
I have five thousand two hundred eighty. *Who has the number of ounces in a pound?*	**I have thirty.** *Who has the number of seconds in a minute?*

Sample Loop C for Grade Four

I have sixty.

Who has the Fahrenheit freezing point of water?

I have one centimeter.

Who has the metric unit of measurement that is equal to one hundred centimeters?

I have thirty-two degrees.

Who has the number of centimeters in three meters?

I have one meter.

Who has the metric unit of measurement that is equal to one thousand meters?

I have three hundred.

Who has the number of meters in five kilometers?

I have a kilometer.

Who has the English unit of measurement for twelve inches?

I have five thousand.

Who has the metric unit of measurement that is 1/100 of a meter?

I have one foot.

Who has the Celsius temperature at which water boils?

Think Math! © 1995 Zephyr Press, Tucson, AZ

Sample Loop D for Grade Four

I have parallel lines.

Who has a line that is flat or parallel to the horizon?

I have radius.

Who has the name of a straight line segment that passes through the center of a circle or sphere?

I have horizontal line.

Who has a line that is at right angles or perpendicular to the horizon?

I have the diameter.

Who has the name for shapes that can be placed exactly on top of each other?

I have vertical line.

Who has lines that move in an oblique direction to the horizon?

I have congruent shapes.

Who has the three-dimensional shape that forms a circle at the base and moves upward until it forms a point at the vertex?

I have slanted lines.

Who has the name of the distance from the center of a circle to the perimeter?

I have a cone.

Who has a three-dimensional shape that is a congruent circle at the top and bottom with sides made up of parallel lines?

Sample Loop D for Grade Four

I have a cylinder.

Who has a three-dimensional surface with all points equidistant from a fixed point?

I have a sphere.

Who has a closed plane figure bounded by three or more line segments?

I have a polygon.

Who has the length of the distance around the outside of a figure?

I have the perimeter.

Who has a number system using the base ten?

I have the decimal system.

Who has the larger of the following decimal numbers: 2.2, 2.12?

I have 2.2.

Who has the smaller of the following decimal numbers: 5.7, 7.5?

I have 5.7.

Who has the decimal equivalent to one-half?

I have .5.

Who has the decimal equivalent to three and three-quarters?

Sample Loop D for Grade Four

I have 3.75.

Who has the decimal equivalent to four-halves?

I have one thousand.

Who has the number of centimeters in a meter?

I have 2.0.

Who has one of the following metric units needed to measure weight: a liter, a gram?

I have one hundred.

Who has the number of deciliters in a liter?

I have a gram.

Who has one of the following metric units needed to measure distance: kilometer, milliliter?

I have ten.

Who has this divided by ten?

I have kilometer.

Who has the number of meters in a kilometer?

I have one.

Who has two or more coplanar lines that do not intersect?

12
Math Loops for Grade Five

The loops in this chapter are not meant to be an accurate list of math skills by grade level for all schools. The math concepts I have used are those most often mentioned for the grade level in Texas's "essential elements." Please use these loops only as a guide or suggestion, not a curriculum outline. Modify and adapt to your own students' abilities, skills, interests, and needs.

Sample Loop A for Grade Five

I have average.

Who has the greater of these numbers: 2,704 and 2,740?

I have >.

Who has the symbol for less than?

I have 2,740.

Who has the lesser of the following numbers: 75,898 and 75,989?

I have <.

Who has a decimal number < one?

I have 75,898.

Who has the symbol for addition?

I have .25.

Who has a fraction that is equivalent to this?

I have +.

Who has the symbol for greater than?

I have 1/4.

Who has the fractional equivalent of three-halves?

Think Math! © 1995 Zephyr Press, Tucson, AZ

Sample Loop A for Grade Five

I have 1 1/2.

Who has the following number: six squared?

I have exponent.

Who has the number that is equivalent to four squared?

I have 6².

Who has a number with an exponent of three?

I have sixteen.

Who has the number equivalent to 7²?

I have 2³.

Who has a whole number that is equivalent to ten cubed?

I have 49.

Who has this divided by 7?

I have one thousand.

What is the name of a number or symbol that denotes the power to which a number is to be raised?

I have seven.

Who has a mixed number that is equivalent to five-halves?

Think Math! © 1995 Zephyr Press, Tucson, AZ

Sample Loop A for Grade Five

I have 2 1/2.

Who has the improper fraction that is equivalent to four and one half?

I have 9/2.

Who has a fractional equivalent to four-sixths?

I have 2/3.

Who has six-tenths reduced to its lowest terms?

I have 3/5.

Who has three-ninths reduced to its lowest terms?

I have 1/3.

Who has one-third plus one-third plus one?

I have 1 2/3.

Who has two-thirds plus one-third?

I have one.

Who has this times one million?

I have 1,000,000.

Who has the number obtained by dividing the sum of a set of quantities by the number of the quantities in the set?

94

Think Math! © 1995 Zephyr Press, Tucson, AZ

Sample Loop B for Grade Five

I have 10.

Who has a number that is one > 501,387?

I have one.

Who has the lowest common denominator of one-half and one-eighth?

I have 501,388.

Who has a number that is one < 501,387?

I have eight.

Who has the lowest common denominator of one-third and one-fifth?

I have 501,386.

Who has the difference between one-half and one-quarter?

I have fifteen.

Who has the lowest denominator of one-seventh and two-fourteenths?

I have ¹/₄.

Who has the difference between 1 ³/₄ and ³/₄?

I have seven.

Who has the product of ¹/₂ times ¹/₃?

Sample Loop B for Grade Five

I have $1/6$. *Who has the product of $2/3$ times $1/2$?*	**I have 3.** *Who has this plus three?*
I have $2/6$. *Who has the name for the number above the line in a fraction?*	**I have six.** *Who has one-third of this?*
I have numerator. *Who has the name for the number below the line in a fraction?*	**I have two.** *Who has eight squared?*
I have denominator. *Who has twenty-one divided by seven?*	**I have sixty-four.** *Who has half of this?*

Think Math! © 1995 Zephyr Press, Tucson, AZ

Sample Loop B for Grade Five

I have thirty-two.

Who has one-eighth of this?

I have 25.

Who has the number of dimes in change when purchasing a $.10 item with a dollar bill?

I have four.

Who has this squared?

I have nine.

Who has the number of gloves necessary to keep the hands of nine children warm on a cold day?

I have 16.

Who has one-fourth of this plus one?

I have 18.

Who has the greater of these two numbers: 88.02 and 88.20?

I have five.

Who has this squared?

I have 88.20.

Who has one-tenth of a hundred?

Think Math! © 1995 Zephyr Press, Tucson, AZ

Sample Loop C for Grade Five

I have protractor. *Who has the Fahrenheit temperature at which water freezes?*	**I have 100°.** *What metric unit would be appropriate to use when measuring the distance between two towns?*
I have 32°. *Who has the Fahrenheit temperature at which water boils?*	**I have kilometer.** *What metric unit would be appropriate to use when measuring the distance from one end of a school hallway to the other?*
I have 212°. *Who has the Celsius temperature at which water freezes?*	**I have meter.** *What metric unit would be appropriate to use when measuring the size of a notebook cover?*
I have 0°. *Who has the Celsius temperature at which water boils?*	**I have centimeter.** *What metric unit would be appropriate to use when measuring the length of a straight pin?*

Sample Loop C for Grade Five

I have millimeter. *What English unit would be appropriate to use when measuring the length of a toothpick?*	**I have feet.** *What English unit would be appropriate to use when measuring the weight of a student?*
I have inch. *What English unit would be appropriate to use when measuring the length of a football field?*	**I have pounds.** *Who has the number of ounces in one pound?*
I have yard. *What English unit would be appropriate to use when measuring the distance between two cities?*	**I have sixteen.** *Who has the metric unit of measure that would be appropriate to use when weighing a student?*
I have mile. *What English unit would be appropriate to use when measuring the size of a classroom?*	**I have kilogram.** *Who has the appropriate unit of English measure to describe the weight of an elephant?*

Think Math! © 1995 Zephyr Press, Tucson, AZ

Sample Loop C for Grade Five

I have ton.

Who has the appropriate unit of English measure to describe the weight of a gerbil?

I have three.

Who has the number of ounces in a quart?

I have ounce.

Who has the appropriate unit of metric measure to describe the weight of a gerbil?

I have 32.

Who has the number of pints in a quart?

I have gram.

Who has the number of quarts in a gallon?

I have two.

Who has the equivalent of two cups?

I have four.

Who has the number of teaspoons in a tablespoon?

I have a pint.

Who has a semi-circular instrument used for measuring and constructing angles?

Sample Loop D for Grade Five

I have an acute angle. *Who has an angle with more than 90°?*	**I have intersecting lines.** *Who has the distance within a circle that is equal to twice the radius?*
I have an obtuse angle. *Who has an angle with 180°?*	**I have the diameter.** *Who has the distance around the outside of a circle?*
I have a straight angle. *Who has an angle with exactly 90°?*	**I have circumference.** *Who has a mathematical instrument that can construct a circle?*
I have a right angle. *Who has the name of two or more lines that cross at the same point?*	**I have a compass.** *Who has a line segment that joins two points on a curve?*

Sample Loop D for Grade Five

I have a chord. *Who has the type of chart that shows relationships of parts to the whole through the use of a circle divided like slices of pie?*	**I have a line graph.** *Who has the results of multiplying the length times the width of a rectangle?*
I have a circle graph. *Who has a chart made up of wide lines that show relationships?*	**I have the area of a rectangle.** *Who has the area of a rectangle that has a length of 10 centimeters and a width of 2 centimeters?*
I have a bar graph. *Who has a chart made up of pictures with each representing a certain value?*	**I have 20 square centimeters.** *Who has a quadrilateral with all sides and all angles equal?*
I have a pictograph. *Who has a chart with many points that are connected?*	**I have a square.** *Who has a quadrilateral with opposite sides parallel but unequal angles?*

Sample Loop D for Grade Five

I have a parallelogram. *Who has the number of quarts in a gallon?*	**I have 100.** *Who has the shapes formed by drawing a straight line between opposite angles of a square?*
I have four. *Who has the number of pints in two gallons?*	**I have triangles.** *Who has the number of sides of an octagon?*
I have sixteen. *Who has the number of grams in a kilogram?*	**I have eight.** *Who has the number of sides of a pentagon?*
I have one thousand. *Who has the number of centimeters in a meter?*	**I have five.** *Who has an angle that has less than 90°?*

13
Math Loops for Grade Six

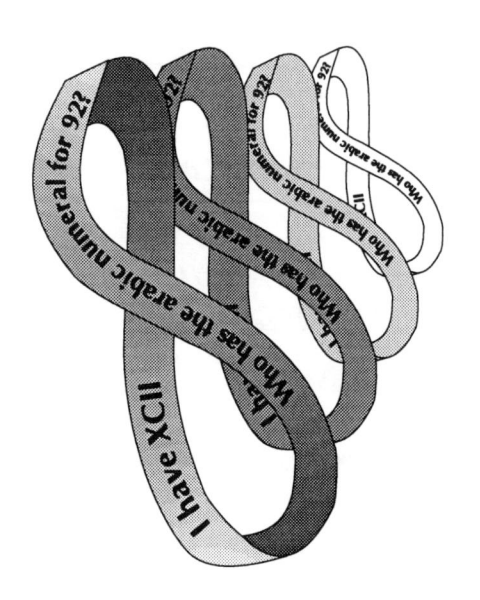

The loops in this chapter are not meant to be an accurate list of math skills by grade level for all schools. The math concepts I have used are those most often mentioned for the grade level in Texas's "essential elements." Please use these loops only as a guide or suggestion, not a curriculum outline. Modify and adapt to your own students' abilities, skills, interests, and needs.

Sample Loop A for Grade Six

I have V. *Who has the roman numeral for 100?*	**I have D.** *Who has the roman numeral for 1000?*
I have C. *Who has the roman numeral for 10?*	**I have M.** *Who has the arabic numeral for LX?*
I have X. *Who has the roman numeral for 50?*	**I have 60.** *Who has the arabic numeral for CC?*
I have L. *Who has the roman numeral for 500?*	**I have 200.** *Who has the arabic numeral for XC?*

Think Math! © 1995 Zephyr Press, Tucson, AZ

Sample Loop A for Grade Six

I have 90.

Who has the arabic numeral for MCC?

I have 1994.

Who has the arabic numeral for MMI?

I have 1200.

Who has the arabic numeral for XVII?

I have 2001.

Who has the arabic numeral for DLV?

I have 17.

Who has the arabic numeral for XXV?

I have 555.

Who has the roman numeral for 92?

I have 25.

Who has the arabic numeral for MCMXCIV?

I have XCII.

Who has the roman numeral for 19?

Sample Loop A for Grade Six

I have XIX. *Who has the roman numeral for 99?*	**I have CCXXII.** *Who has the roman numeral for 18?*
I have XCIX. *Who has the roman numeral for 42?*	**I have XVIII.** *Who has the roman numeral for 21?*
I have XLII. *Who has the roman numeral for 1999?*	**I have XXI.** *Who has the roman numeral for the number of days in a leap year?*
I have MCMXCIX. *Who has the roman numeral for 222?*	**I have CCCLXVI.** *Who has the roman numeral for five?*

Think Math! © 1995 Zephyr Press, Tucson, AZ

Sample Loop B for Grade Six

I have a prime factor. *Who has the least common denominator of 1/3 and 1/4?*	**I have expanded notation.** *Who has the equivalent of 3 x 10?*
I have 12. *Who has the least common denominator of 1/5 and 1/6?*	**I have 30.** *Who has the equivalent of 4×10^2?*
I have 30. *Who has the least common denominator of 2/6 and 8/12?*	**I have 400.** *Who has the equivalent of 8×10^3?*
I have 3. *Who has the term for a number written as the product of a power of ten and a certain numeral?*	**I have 8,000.** *Who has 6.2 x 10?*

Sample Loop B for Grade Six

I have 62. *Who has 19.89 x 100?*	**I have 4,000.** *Who has half of this?*
I have 1989. *Who has 3,333 rounded off to the nearest thousand?*	**I have 2,000.** *Who has one-fourth of this?*
I have 3,000. *Who has 3,511 rounded off to the nearest hundred?*	**I have 500.** *Who has the expanded notation of this?*
I have 3,500. *Who has 3,801 rounded off to the nearest thousand?*	**I have 5×10^2.** *Who has negative 4 minus four more?*

Think Math! © 1995 Zephyr Press, Tucson, AZ

Sample Loop B for Grade Six

I have -8.

Who has the name for the relationship of two quantities as the quotient of one divided by the other?

I have 0.

Who has the number of quarters received in change after buying two $.25 newspapers with a dollar bill?

I have ratio.

Who has the ratio of fifty to one hundred?

I have two.

Who has three-fourths of a dollar?

I have 1:2.

Who has the ratio of forty to sixty?

I have $.75.

Who has two-thirds of this?

I have 2:3.

Who has the product of any number multiplied by zero?

I have $.50.

Who has a numeral that can be divided only by itself and 1?

Sample Loop C for Grade Six

I have 1000. *Who has half of this?*	**I have 3,000.** *Who has the formula for the area of a square?*
I have 500. *Who has one-fifth of this?*	**I have the length of one side squared.** *Who has the area of a square that has one side measuring 20 centimeters in length?*
I have 100. *Who has one-tenth of this?*	**I have 400 square centimeters.** *Who has 350 centimeters plus fifty centimeters?*
I have ten. *Who has 3×10^3?*	**I have 400 centimeters.** *Who has one-fourth of this?*

Think Math! © 1995 Zephyr Press, Tucson, AZ

Sample Loop C for Grade Six

I have one hundred centimeters.

Who has a number that is equivalent to one mile?

I have 5.

Who has this cubed?

I have 5,280 feet.

Who has this plus 20, divided by 53, minus 1?

I have 125.

Who has the term for dividing something exactly in half?

I have 99.

Who has one-third of this?

I have bisect.

Who has a straight line extending from a point?

I have 33.

Who has this plus 3, divided by six, minus one?

I have a ray.

Who has a figure formed by two lines diverging from a single point?

Sample Loop C for Grade Six

I have angle. *Who has another name for average?*	**I have an equilateral triangle.** *Who has a triangle with two equivalent sides?*
I have arithmetic mean. *Who has the average of 80 and 60?*	**I have an isosceles triangle.** *Who has a triangle with three unequal sides?*
I have 70. *Who has the average of 1, 8, and 12?*	**I have a scalene triangle.** *Who has a triangle with one 90-degree angle?*
I have 7. *Who has a figure with three equivalent sides and three equivalent angles?*	**I have a right triangle.** *Who has 10^3?*

Think Math! © 1995 Zephyr Press, Tucson, AZ

Sample Loop D for Grade Six

I have a plane. *Who has a triangle with one angle greater than 90°?*	**I have a hexagon.** *Who has a polyhedron with a square base and triangular faces meeting in a common vertex?*
I have an obtuse triangle. *Who has a triangle with all angles less than 90°?*	**I have a pyramid.** *Who has four minus ten?*
I have an acute triangle. *Who has the name for a four-sided polygon?*	**I have a negative six.** *Who has this plus seven?*
I have a quadrilateral. *Who has a six-sided figure?*	**I have 1.** *Who has this times 6,666,666?*

Sample Loop D for Grade Six

I have 6,666,666.

Who has this times zero?

I have perpendicular.

Who has the number of degrees in a circle?

I have zero.

Who has the number of eighths there are in one inch?

I have 360.

Who has the number of degrees in a triangle?

I have 8.

Who has a dimensionless geometric object having no property but location?

I have 180.

Who has the name for an angle with this same number of degrees?

I have a point.

Who has the word describing a vertical line that extends at a 90° angle from the horizontal base line?

I have a straight angle.

Who has the value of x in the equation 3x = 6?

Sample Loop D for Grade Six

I have 2. *Who has the value of x in the equation 4x + 4 = 16?*	**I have improper fraction.** *Who has a fraction where the denominator is larger than the numerator?*
I have 3. *Who has this squared?*	**I have a proper fraction.** *Who has the place value of the numeral 8 in the following number: 560,080?*
I have nine. *Who has this plus one, times 50?*	**I have the tens place.** *Who has the place value of the numeral 4 in the following number: 540,899?*
I have 500. *Who has a fraction where the numerator is larger than the denominator?*	**I have the ten thousands place.** *Who has a surface containing all the straight lines connecting any two points on it?*

14
Math Loops for Grades Seven and Eight

The loops in this chapter are not meant to be an accurate list of math skills by grade level for all schools. The math concepts I have used are those most often mentioned for the grade level in Texas's "essential elements." Please use these loops only as a guide or suggestion, not a curriculum outline. Modify and adapt to your own students' abilities, skills, interests, and needs.

Sample Loop A for Grades Seven and Eight

I have probability.

Who has the likelihood of one dot appearing when one die is rolled?

I have the median.

Who has the probability of heads appearing when a coin is flipped?

I have one out of six.

Who has the likelihood of one dot appearing when two dice are rolled?

I have one out of two.

In the number 5,823, who has the name of the place occupied by the five?

I have two out of six or one out of three.

Who has the most frequently observed number in a series of numbers?

I have the thousands place.

Who has the place occupied by the four in the following number: fourteen hundred ninety-two?

I have the mode.

Who has the middle number in a series of numbers?

I have the hundreds place.

Who has the approximate value of pi (π)?

Sample Loop A for Grades Seven and Eight

I have 3.14.

If light travels at 186,281.7 miles per second, who has this number rounded off to the nearest thousand miles per second?

I have three and two and one.

Who has the list of negative numbers greater than negative four?

I have 186,000.

If a tape cassette costs $10.11 including tax, who has the estimate of what a dozen cassettes would cost?

I have -3, -2, -1.

Who has all the integers between minus two and plus two?

I have $120 dollars.

If a set of four new tires for an all terrain vehicle costs eight hundred twelve dollars, who has the estimated price of one?

I have -1, 0, and +1.

Who has the decimal equivalent to one-half?

I have $200 dollars.

Who has the list of whole numbers less than four?

I have five tenths (.5).

Who has the decimal equivalent to three-fourths?

Think Math! © 1995 Zephyr Press, Tucson, AZ

Sample Loop A for Grades Seven and Eight

I have seventy-five hundredths (.75).

Who has the whole number equivalent to four halves?

I have two.

Who has the heavier of two gerbils if one weighs two and three-tenths ounces and one weighs two and one-fourth ounces?

I have two and three-tenths ounces.

Who has the lighter of two earthworms if one weighs three-eighths of an ounce and one weighs half an ounce?

I have three-eighths of an ounce.

Who has a fraction that is equivalent to six-eighths and twelve-sixteenths?

I have three-fourths.

Who has the word name for the number one followed by six zeros (1,000,000)?

I have one million.

Who has the word name for the number one followed by twelve zeros?

I have one trillion.

Who has the word name for the number one followed by nine zeros?

I have one billion.

Who has the number expressing the likelihood of the occurrence of a specific event in the form of a ratio?

Sample Loop B for Grades Seven and Eight

I have one billion.

Who has the scientific notation for the following decimal: 340.67?

I have 100.

Who has 25% of this?

I have 3.4067×10^2.

Who has the decimal notation for the following: 4.86×10^3?

I have 25.

Who has 50% of $100.00?

I have 4,860.

Who has the symbol for percent?

I have $50.00.

Who has the percent equivalent of the decimal .75?

I have %.

Who has 10% of 1,000?

I have 75%.

Who has the fractional equivalent of this?

Think Math! © 1995 Zephyr Press, Tucson, AZ

Sample Loop B for Grades Seven and Eight

I have three-fourths.

Who has the decimal equivalent of this?

I have 6 x 10^{-2}.

Who has half of this?

I have seventy-five hundredths (.75).

Who has thirty-three and one-third percent of this?

I have three one-hundredths.

Who has the number of centimeters in one-third of a meter stick?

I have twenty-five hundredths (.25).

Who has the equivalent to 4 x 10^{-3}?

I have thirty-three and one-third centimeters.

Who has 50% of the meters in a kilometer?

I have four one-thousandths (.004).

Who has the scientific notation for six one-hundredths?

I have five hundred meters.

Who has 50% of a meter stick?

Sample Loop B for Grades Seven and Eight

I have fifty centimeters. *Who has three-fourths of a kilometer?*	**I have 2,000 pounds.** *Who has the number of pints in a quart?*
I have 750 meters. *Who has double this?*	**I have two pints.** *Who has the number of quarts in a gallon?*
I have 1,500 meters. *Who has thirty-three and one-third percent of this plus one?*	**I have 4 quarts.** *Who has the number of pints in a gallon?*
I have five hundred one meters. *Who has the number of pounds in a short ton?*	**I have eight pints.** *Who has the word name for 10^9?*

Think Math! © 1995 Zephyr Press, Tucson, AZ

Sample Loop C for Grades Seven and Eight

I have sixteen ounces. *Who has the number of inches in a yard?*	**I have 1,000.** *Who has the number of kilograms in 1,000 grams?*
I have thirty-six inches. *Who has the number of feet in a mile?*	**I have one.** *Who has the formula for the area of a rectangle?*
I have 5,280 feet. *Who has the number of inches in a foot?*	**I have area = length times width.** *Who has the value of x in the equation x + 2 = 4?*
I have twelve inches. *Who has the number of milliliters in a liter?*	**I have two.** *Who has the space inside a three-dimensional, or solid, figure?*

Sample Loop C for Grades Seven and Eight

I have volume.

Who has the horizontal number line in a coordinate graph?

I have 10^{-1}.

Who has the point of intersection of the sides of an angle?

I have x-axis.

Who has the word that describes the cutting off of a number at a particular decimal place?

I have vertex.

Who has a variable that is to be solved for an equation?

I have truncate.

Who has the cost of the given unit of an object?

I have unknown.

Who has the name of a four-sided polygon?

I have unit cost.

Who has the equivalent of one-tenth?

I have a quadrilateral.

Who has the name of one of the four parts into which the coordinate plane is divided by the x-axis and the y-axis?

Think Math! © 1995 Zephyr Press, Tucson, AZ

Sample Loop C for Grades Seven and Eight

I have quadrant.

Who has the word that means a turn of 360 degrees?

I have a prime number.

Who has a chart in which information is represented using a circle that has been cut into sectors to show values of a particular category?

I have revolution.

Who has half of a circle?

I have a pie graph or circle graph.

Who has the name given to rays, segments, or lines that form right angles?

I have semicircle.

Who has the equivalent of one-sixteenth of a pound?

I have perpendicular.

Who has an event with the possibility of zero?

I have an ounce.

Who has a positive integer whose only positive integer divisors are itself and one?

I have an impossible event.

Who has the number of ounces in a pint?

Sample Loop D for Grades Seven and Eight

I have 2000 square yards.

Who has the area of a table that is six feet long and three feet wide?

I have 18 square feet.

Who has the area of a sliding glass door that is six feet tall and nine feet wide?

I have 54 square feet.

Who has the surface area of a box that is 10 inches long, 5 inches wide, and 2 inches deep?

I have 160 square inches.

Who has the surface area of a pizza box that is ten inches long, ten inches wide, and one inch deep?

I have 240 square inches.

Who has the volume of a shoe box that is 5 inches high, 5 inches wide, and 10 inches long?

I have 250 cubic inches.

Who has the volume of a cube with 2 feet on each side?

I have 8 cubic feet.

Who has the volume of a trunk that is 3 feet wide, 5 feet long, and 2 feet deep?

I have 30 cubic feet.

Who has the perimeter of a rectangle 12 feet long and 2 feet wide?

Sample Loop D for Grades Seven and Eight

I have 28 feet.

Who has the perimeter of a triangle that has two sides 8 inches long and a third side 10 inches long?

I have 4.

Who has one-third of 27?

I have 26 inches.

Who has the perimeter of a field that is one mile long and a half mile wide?

I have 9.

Who has one-fourth of 40?

I have 3 miles.

Who has the product of one-third times one-half?

I have 10.

Who has double this, plus one?

I have one-sixth.

Who has one-half times eight?

I have 21.

Who has one-third of this?

128

Think Math! © 1995 Zephyr Press, Tucson, AZ

Sample Loop D for Grades Seven and Eight

I have 7.

Who has this squared?

I have thirty.

Who has six more than this?

I have 49.

Who has one more than this, plus 25?

I have thirty-six.

Who has the square root of this?

I have 75.

Who has double this?

I have 6.

Who has this times a negative two?

I have 150.

Who has one-fifth of this?

I have -12.

Who has the area of a field that is 100 yards long and 20 yards wide?

Sample Loop E for Grades Seven and Eight

I have lb. *Who has the abbreviation for foot?*	**I have qt.** *Who has the abbreviation for gallon?*
I have ft. *Who has the abbreviation for mile?*	**I have gal.** *Who has the abbreviation for kilometer?*
I have mi. *Who has the abbreviation for yard?*	**I have km.** *Who has the abbreviation for meter?*
I have yd. *Who has the abbreviation for quart?*	**I have m.** *Who has the abbreviation for kilogram?*

Sample Loop E for Grades Seven and Eight

I have kg.

Who has the abbreviation for milligram?

I have ml.

Who has the number of centimeters in a meter?

I have mg.

Who has the abbreviation for centimeter?

I have 100.

Who has the number of meters in 216 centimeters?

I have cm.

Who has the abbreviation for millimeter?

I have 2.16 meters.

Who has the number of cents in $3.40?

I have mm.

Who has the abbreviation for milliliter?

I have 340 cents.

Who has the number of millimeters in one meter?

Think Math! © 1995 Zephyr Press, Tucson, AZ

131

Sample Loop E for Grades Seven and Eight

I have 1000.

Who has one-billionth of a second?

I have 2000.

Who has the percentage of a meter that one centimeter is?

I have a nanosecond.

Who has one-thousandth of a second?

I have one percent.

Who has the number of grams in three kilograms?

I have a millisecond.

Who has the number of cents in $5?

I have 3000.

Who has the equivalent fraction of .125?

I have 500.

Who has the number of milliliters in two liters?

I have one-eighth.

Who has the abbreviation for pound?

132

Think Math! © 1995 Zephyr Press, Tucson, AZ

Sample Loop F for Grades Seven and Eight

I have 71%.

Who has 7 out of 50 written as a percent?

I have 55%.

Who has the number of games a team won if they played 16 games and won 25%?

I have 14%.

Who has 1 out of 10 written as a percent?

I have 4.

Who has the number of games a team lost if they played 16 games and lost 50%?

I have 10%.

Who has 14 out of 14 written as a percent?

I have 8.

Who has the number of games a team tied if they played 20 games and tied 10% of their games?

I have 100%.

Who has 11 out of 20 written as a percent?

I have 2.

Who has the number of games a team won if they played 20 games and lost 10% of them?

Think Math! © 1995 Zephyr Press, Tucson, AZ

Sample Loop F for Grades Seven and Eight

I have 18.

Who has the number of games a team lost if they played 20 games and won 50% of their games?

I have $.10.

Who has the tax owed on $10.00 if the rate is 8%?

I have 10.

Who has the percentage of games a team won if they lost 10% of their games?

I have eighty cents.

Who has the percentage of students that passed a test if $3/4$ of them passed?

I have 90%.

Who has the percentage of games a team lost if they won 85% of their games?

I have 75%.

Who has the number of colors missing from a crayon box of eight if $3/4$ of the crayons are gone?

I have 15%.

Who has the tax owed on $2.00 if the rate is 5%?

I have 6.

Who has the fraction that is equivalent to 20%?

Sample Loop F for Grades Seven and Eight

I have $^1/_5$. *Who has a fraction that is equivalent to 60%?*	**I have** $^4/_5$. *Who has the lesser value, 80% or .75?*
I have $^6/_{10}$. *Who has the decimal equivalent to 7.5%?*	**I have .75.** *Who has the number of people in a stadium if it holds 2000 people and it is 50% empty?*
I have .075. *Who has the decimal equivalent to 70%?*	**I have 1000.** *Who has the number of people in a stadium if it holds 10,000 people and it is 80% full?*
I have .7. *Who has the greater value, $^4/_5$ or 75%?*	**I have 8,000.** *Who has 71 out of 100, written as a percent?*

Think Math! © 1995 Zephyr Press, Tucson, AZ

Sample Loop G for Grades Seven and Eight

I have $^1/_2$.

Who has a ratio that is equal to the fraction $^1/_{10}$?

I have 4.

Who has 75% of 12?

I have 1:10.

Who has the fraction that is equal to the ratio of 1:6?

I have 9.

Who has the fractional equivalent of 33%?

I have $^2/_{12}$.

Who has a ratio that is equal to the fraction $^{25}/_{50}$?

I have one-third.

Who has the percent of increase of an item that went from $300.00 to $450.00?

I have 1:2.

Who has 25% of 16?

I have 50%.

Who has the percent of decrease of an item that went from $10.00 down to $7.50?

136

Think Math! © 1995 Zephyr Press, Tucson, AZ

Sample Loop G for Grades Seven and Eight

I have 25%. *Who has the solution to the value of b in the following equation: 3b = 90?*	**I have $50.00.** *Who has the inverse operation to subtraction?*
I have b = 30. *Who has the solution to the value of b in the following equation: 2b = 90?*	**I have addition.** *Who has the inverse operation to division?*
I have b = 45. *Who has the solution to the value of b in the following equation: 4 + b = 24?*	**I have multiplication.** *Who has a number sentence with an equal sign in it?*
I have b = 20. *Who has 25% of $200.00?*	**I have an equation.** *Who has the value of y if 3y = 18?*

Think Math! © 1995 Zephyr Press, Tucson, AZ

Sample Loop G for Grades Seven and Eight

I have six.

Who has the value of y if 2y = 48?

I have 2(11 x 5).

Who has an expression that means five more than twice a number y?

I have 24.

Who has a value that can change?

I have 2y + 5.

Who has an expression that means 16 decreased by a number r?

I have a variable.

Who has an expression that means three less than a number x?

I have 16 - r.

Who has an expression that means a number n squared, then divided by 5?

I have x - 3.

Who has an expression that means twice the product of 11 and 5?

I have $n^2 \div 5$.

Who has a fraction that is equal to a ratio of 20:40?

Think Math! © 1995 Zephyr Press, Tucson, AZ

15
Geometry Loops

This chapter contains two loops with geometry terms and concepts. Each loop has twenty-four cards that you can copy, cut apart, and distribute to students. Please use these loops only as a guide or suggestion, not a curriculum outline. Modify and adapt to your own students' abilities, skills, interests, and needs.

Geometry Loop A

I have space.

Who has the name of all points in a line?

I have seven.

Who has the name for two objects that have the same size and shape?

I have collinear points.

Who has the set of points that two lines have in common?

I have congruent.

Who has the name of an angle that measures between 0° and 90°?

I have intersection.

Who has the value of the variable in the equation 8 + C = 13?

I have an acute angle.

Who has the name of an angle that measures between 90° and 180°?

I have five.

Who has the variable in the equation 42 = 6K?

I have an obtuse angle.

Who has an angle that measures exactly 90°?

Geometry Loop A

I have a right angle. *Who has an angle that measures exactly 180°?*	**I have postulates.** *Who has two angles whose sum equals 90°?*
I have a straight angle. *Who has the exact number of lines there can be through two points?*	**I have complementary angles.** *Who has two angles whose sum equals 180°?*
I have one. *Who has the word for statements that are true?*	**I have supplementary angles.** *Who has the term for two angles in which the sides of one angle are opposite rays to the sides of the other angle?*
I have theorems. *Who has the word for statements that are accepted without proof?*	**I have vertical angles.** *Who has the name for two lines that form congruent adjacent angles?*

Geometry Loop A

I have perpendicular lines.

Who has the name for coplanar lines that do not intersect?

I have an equiangular triangle.

Who has a triangle with each angle less than 90°?

I have parallel lines.

Who has the name for lines that are not parallel and do not intersect?

I have an acute triangle.

Who has a figure formed by three segments joining three noncollinear points?

I have skew lines.

Who has a triangle with no sides congruent?

I have a triangle.

Who has a triangle with at least two congruent sides?

I have a scalene triangle.

Who has a triangle with all angles congruent?

I have an isosceles triangle.

Who has the set of all points?

Geometry Loop B

I have a right triangle.

Who has a triangle with all sides congruent?

I have altitude.

Who has the segment of a line that is perpendicular to the segment at its midpoint?

I have an equilateral triangle.

Who has the number of degrees in each of its angles?

I have a perpendicular bisector.

Who has a statement that is accepted without proof?

I have 60°.

Who has the segment of a triangle from a vertex to the midpoint of the opposite side?

I have an axiom.

Who has an angle with its vertex at the center of the circle?

I have median.

Who has a perpendicular segment of a triangle from a vertex to the line that contains the opposite side?

I have a central angle of a circle.

Who has a line segment whose end points lie on a circle?

Think Math! © 1995 Zephyr Press, Tucson, AZ

Geometry Loop B

I have a chord. *Who has the perimeter of a circle?*	**I have a cube.** *Who has a ten-sided polygon?*
I have circumference. *Who has the name for circles that lie in the same plane and have the same center?*	**I have a decagon.** *Who has a chord that contains the center of a circle?*
I have concentric circles. *Who has the name for arcs in the same circle with equal measurements?*	**I have diameter.** *Who has a segment joining two nonconsecutive vertices of a polygon?*
I have congruent arcs. *Who has a rectangular solid with square faces?*	**I have a diagonal.** *Who has an equation whose graph is a line?*

Think Math! © 1995 Zephyr Press, Tucson, AZ

Geometry Loop B

I have a linear equation. *Who has the name of the side opposite the right angle in a right triangle?*	**I have proportion.** *Who has a quadrilateral with four right angles?*
I have the hypotenuse. *Who has an equation for the area of a circle?*	**I have a rectangle.** *Who has a quadrilateral with four congruent sides?*
I have $A = \pi r^2$. *Who has an equation for the circumference of a circle?*	**I have a rhombus.** *Who has the two arcs of a circle that are cut off by the diameter?*
I have $C = \pi d$. *Who has an equation that states that two ratios are equal?*	**I have semicircles.** *Who has a triangle with one angle equal to 90°?*

Think Math! © 1995 Zephyr Press, Tucson, AZ

16
Algebra Loops

This chapter contains two loops with algebra terms and concepts. Each loop has twenty-four cards that you can copy, cut apart, and distribute to students. Please use these loops only as a guide or suggestion, not a curriculum outline. Modify and adapt to your own students' abilities, skills, interests, and needs.

Algebra Loop A

I have n = 4. *Who has the value of n if 6n = 30?*	**I have x = 1.** *Who has the value of n if 4 - 2 = n?*
I have n = 5. *Who has the value of x if 3/4x = 12?*	**I have n = 2.** *Who has the value of x if x - 7 = 10?*
I have x = 16. *Who has the value of n if 2n = 12?*	**I have x = 17.** *Who has the value of x if 2/3x = 10?*
I have n = 6. *Who has the value of x if 12x = 12?*	**I have x = 15.** *Who has the value of x if 1/2x = 3?*

Algebra Loop A

I have x = 6.

Who has the value of n if 6 + n = 20?

I have n = 8.

Who has the value of x if 50x = 100?

I have n = 14.

Who has the value of x if 4x + 1 = 13?

I have x = 2.

Who has the value of n if 4 - n = 4?

I have x = 3.

Who has the value of n if (4)(5) = n?

I have n = 0.

Who has the value of n if six times eight equals n?

I have n = 20.

Who has the value of n if twenty-four divided by three equals n?

I have n = 48.

Who has the value of n if 1/2n = 150?

Algebra Loop A

I have n = 300. *Who has the value of x if 100/4 = x?*	**I have n = 30.** *Who has the value of x if 1/4x = 100?*
I have x = 25. *Who has the value of n if n + 1 = 71?*	**I have x = 400.** *Who has the value of n if 42/n = 2?*
I have n = 70. *Who has the value of n if 2n = 100?*	**I have n = 21.** *Who has the value of n if 3n = 21?*
I have n = 50. *Who has the value of n if 3n = 90?*	**I have n = 7.** *Who has the value of n if one-half of n equals two?*

Think Math! © 1995 Zephyr Press, Tucson, AZ

Algebra Loop B

I have 24. Who has the value of n + 15, if n = 1?	**I have 18.** Who has the value of b - 10, if b = 5?
I have 16. Who has the value of b + 10, if b = 5?	**I have -5.** Who has the value of b - 10, if b = 50?
I have 15. Who has the value of b + 10, if b = 20?	**I have 40.** Who has the value of n + 10, if n = 4?
I have 30. Who has the value of b + 10, if b = 8?	**I have 14.** Who has the value of b + 20, if b = 25?

Algebra Loop B

I have 45.

Who has the value of (b)(10), if b = 8?

I have 48.

Who has the value of 4n, if n = .5?

I have 80.

Who has the value of n/2, if n = 5?

I have 2.

Who has the value of 4n, if n = -8?

I have two and one-half.

Who has the value of 4n, if n = 8?

I have a negative 32.

Who has the value of 10n, if n = .10?

I have 32.

Who has the value of 6n, if n = 8?

I have one.

Who has a number that is 3 > 6?

Algebra Loop B

I have 9.

Who has a number that is
4 < 12?

I have 36°.

Who has a temperature that is
10° < 6°?

I have 8.

Who has a number that is
2 < 1 ?

I have -4°.

Who can simplify -(-3.1)?

I have -1.

Who has a number that is
5 < -5?

I have 3.1.

Who can simplify (4)(-4)?

I have -10.

Who has a temperature that is
4° > 32°?

I have -16.

Who can simplify (-4)(-6)?

152

Think Math! © 1995 Zephyr Press, Tucson, AZ

EXTRA! EXTRA!
YOUR STUDENTS CAN'T WAIT TO TAKE THIS MAGICAL MYSTERY TOUR!

A MATHEMATICAL MYSTERY TOUR
Higher-Thinking Math Tasks
by Mark Wahl
Grades 5–12

Now you can integrate art, science, philosophy, history, social studies, and language arts. The required Mystery Tour Guide newspaper integrates with each unit, adding questions, activities, puzzles, and tidbits of mathematical information. You'll receive a sample newspaper with the purchase of each book. Order additional newspapers in sets of five. Students should have their own newspapers, or if funds are limited, 3–4 students may share.

A MATHEMATICAL MYSTERY TOUR (Book)
256-page book, 8 1/2" x 11", softbound; with sample newspaper.
BOOK—1006-W . . . $24.95

MYSTERY TOUR GUIDE NEWSPAPER
PLEASE NOTE: This follow-along newspaper accompanies the book. One copy is recommended for each participant. 16-page tabloid, 11" x 17".
SET OF FIVE NEWSPAPERS—1007-W . . . $9.95

WHAT NEXT?
Futuristic Scenarios for Creative Problem Solving
by Robert E. Myers and E. Paul Torrance
Grades 6–12

Tap into students' natural interest in the future with writing activities you can incorporate into language arts, social studies, or humanities programs. Select from 52 exciting units to nourish creative thinking and to inspire thinking about the future.

388 pages, 8 1/2" x 11", softbound.
1049-W . . . $35

CALL, WRITE, OR FAX FOR YOUR FREE CATALOG!

ORDER FORM
☎ Please include your phone number in case we have questions about your order.

Qty.	Item #	Title	Unit Price	Total
	1006-W	A Mathematical Mystery Tour	$24.95	
	1049-W	What Next	$35	

Name _____
Address _____
City _____
State _____ Zip _____
Phone (_____) _____

Method of payment (check one):
❑ Check or Money Order   ❑ Visa
❑ MasterCard   ❑ Purchase Order attached
Credit Card No. _____
Expires _____
Signature _____

Subtotal
Sales Tax (AZ residents, 5%)
S & H (10% of Subtotal-min $3.00)
Total (U.S. Funds only)

CANADA: add 22% for S&H and G.S.T.

100% SATISFACTION GUARANTEE
Upon receiving your order you'll have 30 days of risk-free evaluation. If you are not 100% satisfied, return your order within 30 days for a 100% refund of the purchase price. No questions asked!

To order write or call:

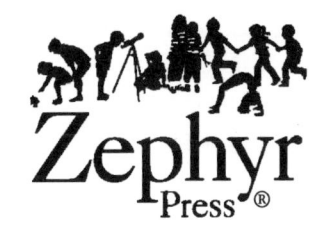

Zephyr Press®
REACHING THEIR HIGHEST POTENTIAL

P.O. Box 66006-W
Tucson, AZ 85728-6006

(520) 322-5090
FAX (520) 323-9402